Janet Borsbey | Ruth Swan

Crossing Cultures

Lessons about the English-Speaking World

Teacher's Book

ELI

Crossing Cultures
Janet Borsbey
Ruth Swan

Project Management: Sarah Howell
Project Development: Cristiana Papi
Eli Editorial Dept.: Maria Cristina Izzo, Marco Mercatali
Eli Design Dept.: Enea Ciccarelli

Cover
Graphic Design: P. Lorenzetti
Photo: Masterfile

© 2007 **ELI** s.r.l.
P.O. Box 6
62019 Recanati
Italy
Tel. +39 071 750701
Fax. +39 071 977851
e-mail: info@elionline.com
www.elionline.com

No unauthorised photocopying

All rights reserved. No part of this publication may be reproduced, stored in a retrieval system, or transmitted, in any form or by any means, electronic, mechanical, photocopying, recording or otherwise, without the prior written permission of ELI.

This book is sold subject to the condition that it shall not, by way of trade or otherwise, be lent, resold, hired out, or otherwise circulated without the publisher's prior consent in any form of binding or cover other than that in which it is published and without a similar condition including this condition being imposed on the subsequent purchaser.

ISBN 9788853610867
Printed in Italy by Tecnostampa - 07.83.243.0

All websites referred to in Crossing Cultures are in public domain and, whilst every effort has been made to check that the websites were current at the time of going to press, Eli s.r.l disclaims responsibility for their content and/or possible changes.

While every effort has been made to trace all the copyright holders, if any have been inadvertently overlooked the publishers will be pleased to make the necessary arrangements at the first opportunity.

Contents

Introduction p. 4

Table of contents p. 10

Teacher's notes p. 12

Photocopiable materials p. 76

Tests p. 81

Answers to tests p. 92

CD-ROM Keys p. 94

Introduction

In a multi-national, multi-cultural context, culture studies takes on a renewed importance in schools. To understand and produce a language, students need a cultural framework as well as grounding in skills, vocabulary and grammar. This book takes a fresh look at culture studies in English, via a journey through the English-speaking world, exploding a few myths along the way! The book is flexible and addresses traditional culture studies topics as well as some newer concepts. The underlying aim of the book is to equip students with the tools they need to begin to understand the English-speaking world through its variety of language and culture. Systematic skills development and ample opportunities for cross-curricular links make the book rewarding and stimulating for students.

Who it is for

The book is intended for use in secondary schools and has been designed with careful reference to *The Common European Framework of Reference for Languages* as well as national syllabus requirements.

Key Features of the Book

Approach to Culture Studies

We have interpreted culture studies as referring to the English-speaking world. As a result the course contains the main geographical, historical and biographical information needed to get an overview of the principal English-speaking nations. In addition to these traditional areas, the aim has been to give students more of an insight into cultural references students meet in films, TV programmes and when listening to music. For this reason, there is also material on subjects as varied as the Thanksgiving turkey, school lockers and charity wristbands.

Flexibility

The structure of the book has been carefully planned to allow teachers a choice in how to use the material. Teachers can work through the book in order, pick and choose individual lessons which fit in with topics from their main course book or choose to do a selection of lessons from any one of the five main topic headings. In addition, there are a number of suggested alternative routes in this Teacher's Book. Many activities in the book are open-ended. This allows all students of varying levels and abilities to make a meaningful contribution to the lesson.

Cross-curricular links

Most of the lessons contain a cross-curricular element. Culture Studies as a subject naturally lends itself to links with other disciplines such as geography and history. In addition, this book provides openings for cooperation with teachers from subjects such as, for example, maths (with charts, graphs, tables and mental arithmetic), science (with regular experiments in the Chill Zone and many lessons in Block E of a scientific nature), religion (with comparative studies from the ESW) and citizenship (with topics such as immigration). Students find this type of cross-curricular link fascinating and motivating and it ensures that culture studies caters for students with different interests, abilities and intelligences.

Skills development

Speaking
The development of productive skills is addressed in each lesson through an **Over to You** section at the end of each lesson, where students are encouraged to work in pairs and small groups. Most **Warm-up** activities are oral, and students are given opportunities to express their own opinions actively throughout the lessons with short personalization activities in **Your Turn**.

Writing
Writing activities are designed to develop students' skills in line with descriptors in the *Common European Framework of Reference for Languages*. The activities are integrated into the **Over to You** section and include writing postcards, letters, emails, signs and notices and short reports. Alternative homework writing suggestions are offered in this Teacher's Book. Summary skills are developed via the **Working with Texts** sections.

Reading
Reading activities are also designed to develop global and specific skills. In addition, the **Working with Texts** sections contain extra comprehension and summary skills work. In the lessons, students meet texts from magazines, newspapers, brochures, text books, guide books, labels and websites.

Listening
A variety of listening activities is included, so that students work on developing global and specific listening skills in different contexts. Students listen to interviews, dialogues, conversations, monologues and excerpts from TV & radio programmes in a variety of accents which are representative of the English spoken all over the world. Where appropriate, the speakers' accents are indicated next to the audio script using the abbreviations listed below.

Key to accents

Carib = Caribbean
Eng = English
N. Eng = Northern English (e.g. Lancashire, Yorkshire)
S. Eng = Southern English (e.g. Essex, London)
GB = British (e.g. could be slight, almost unnoticeable Scottish or Irish)
Scot = Scottish
USA = American
Irish
Can = Canadian
NZ = New Zealand
Aus = Australian
Ind = Indian

Approach to international examinations

As many schools now offer students the opportunity to take internationally-recognised examinations, Crossing Cultures addresses this issue by providing activities which help in preparation for examinations from boards such as Cambridge ESOL and Trinity Examinations. These are clearly flagged in the Student's Book.

Components

Student's Book
2 Audio CD ROMs
Teacher's Book

The Student's Book

The student's book is divided into 10 blocks. Each block contains:

a) 5 lessons, one each about the following:

In and Out of School
People and Daily Life
Sport and Leisure
National Identity
Our World

Each lesson is on a double-page spread and takes from 45 to 55 minutes. Suggestions for short-cuts and extension are given in this Teacher's Book. Lessons progress in language and vocabulary difficulty from Block 1 to Block 10. They also progress in terms of the maturity needed to approach the topics, and in terms of the tasks students are asked to complete.

b) The Chill Zone
This is designed as a fun space where students can 'chill' in English, with games, songs, jokes and puzzles etc. They relate loosely to the topics explored in the previous five lessons, but can also be used at other moments, perhaps when the class needs some light relief.

c) Working with Texts
This double page at the end of each block contains a longer text for teachers who are working on comprehension and summary activities. The texts are related to one of the topic areas in the five main lessons, but stand alone. The activities are designed to teach the skills students need to prepare for their state examinations.

Separately from these blocks you will find:

a) ESW Profiles
At the end of the book, students will find 7 **Profiles on...**These dossiers contain factual encyclopaedic information about Australia & New Zealand, the Commonwealth, the UK, Ireland, India, The USA and Canada. They are intended for use as an active reference section.

b) Word list and glossary

The Teacher's Book

- Full answer key
- Audio-scripts integrated into the key
- Supplementary activities, shortcuts and tips
- Homework suggestions
- Alternatives routes through the book
- Extra cultural input
- Detailed objectives
- Suggested websites
- Error prediction in pronunciation, language and vocabulary use
- Photocopiable worksheets
- Tests

Alternatives routes through the book

As stated above, one of our main aims has been to create material which is flexible enough to allow teachers and students to choose different routes through the book. Here are some of our suggestions of possible routes:

Chronological

Some teachers may have time to integrate Crossing Cultures with their course book and so work through lessons in the order in which they appear in the book. The material has been graded in order to offer progression in terms of language items and lexical difficulty. Material has also been ordered in terms of maturity; topics such as government and music are covered in the second half of the book. Teachers who use this approach should bear in mind that there is no thematic link between lessons, so each double-page spread should be regarded as a separate lesson.

Block by block

Rather than moving chronologically through the book, some teachers may prefer to use the general topic groupings to approach the material. An example of this could be to complete all the lessons in Section B, the **People and Daily Life** section. This would involve the following:

1B Chores, Chores, Chores: jobs children do at home
lexis of chores, listening for specific information, quiz on chores, reading & true / false, maths problem, speaking: assigning chores

2B Food, glorious food: food and drink
lexis of school lunches, listening for specific information, reading & ordering cartoon, citizenship, speaking: discussion of irritating habits

3B My Room: bedroom and bathroom culture
lexis of bedrooms and bathrooms, reading for specific information, citizenship, speaking: redesigning task

4B Saturday Jobs: kids who work
lexis of Saturday jobs, listening for gist, the law, reading & true / false, speaking: organizing a special event

5B Tea time: family mealtimes
lexis of mealtimes & food, reading: gist and specific, listening for specific information, cultural differences, quiz, speaking: decision-making

6B Home Sweet Home: types of homes
lexis of homes and rooms, listening for gist, reading & matching, maths task, speaking: advantages and disadvantages discussion

7B Life then and life now: daily life in the past and today
lexis of household objects, reading: spot the anachronism, product design, reading & true / false, web project on design, speaking: plan a high-tech house

8B Town and Country: village, small town and city life
lexis of towns and the countryside, reading & extrapolating advantages and disadvantages, listening for specific information, citizenship, speaking: planning and budgeting a trip in a big city, writing: a postcard

9B Praise Be! religion and worship
lexis of religious buildings and symbols, reading a pie chart, reading & matching, reading & ordering, writing: stories and fables

10B Culture within a culture: the Amish and Native Americans
reading & matching FAQs, history, listening for specific information, speaking: reasoning about animal tracks

Using the Section B route on **People and Daily Life**, learners still have access to a wide variety of exercise types, skills activities and cross-curricular elements and progression is still evident in terms of moving from personal to more abstract issues.

Project/CLIL-style approach

Crossing Cultures can also be used as a mine of information for teachers who prefer to organize culture studies projects at different stages throughout the school year or teachers who have the opportunity to work with colleagues from different disciplines. In our view, culture studies offers the perfect opportunity for this type of methodology. A full example of this approach follows:

Europe and the New World: navigation, discovery, colonization and immigration

Warm-up: copy a pre-Columbus map of the world and ask students to mark differences between it and today's map.

Stage One: Navigation and Discovery of America.
Lesson 7D The Age of Discovery; The Chill Zone 7.

- Students brainstorm great navigators **7D Warm-up**
- Students follow Columbus' route on a map from reading a text **7D ex 1**
- Students use their general knowledge and imagination to decide what items navigators brought back from the new world **7D Your Turn**
- Focus students attention on the information about knots **7D Did you know?** (skip ex 2 for the moment)
- Students learn about latitude and navigation **7D ex 3**
- Task: Students make their own quadrant (photocopy in this Teacher's Book) **7D ex 3**
- Task: Students use their quadrants to learn how Columbus navigated **7D ex 3**
- Warm down with discussion on difficulties navigators faced
- Discuss the world being considered flat **Chill Zone 7 Explode the Myth!**
- Students re-order The Columbus Rap and use it to help them learn or revise the information about Columbus **The Chill Zone 7**

Stage Two: Discovery of Australia & New Zealand.
Lesson 7D The Age of Discovery.

- Compare the dates for Columbus' voyage to America and Captain Cook's voyages to map Australasia **7D ex 2**
- Focus on the map of present day Australia and New Zealand in the **Profile on Australia and New Zealand**

Stage Three: Colonization of indigenous populations

- Students find out about Maoris **CD Rom reading text**
- Students find out about Aborigine culture **9B ex 3**
- Students find out about Native Americans and Cherokee culture **10B ex 2** and **Explode the Myth!**
- Task: students use a Native American skill: tracking **10B Over to You**
- Warm down with discussion of the effects of European colonization on the indigenous populations

Stage Four: Later Immigration from Europe into the USA and Australia

- Students read about the Pilgrim Fathers **Working with Texts 9**
- Students read about C20 immigration into the USA **Working with Texts 6**
- Task: students complete a landing card from Ellis Island **6D Your Turn**
- Students learn about immigration into Australia **6D Warm-up, ex 1**
- task: students plan their journey as immigrants **6D Over to You**

Final stage: students produce a diary of their personal journey into the New World.

Each of the above stages could be used as a stand-alone project.

A selection of other Project-CLIL routes:

The history of the UK

Profile page158
4D Origins of English
6A What did you get?

Chill Zone 6 Domesday
9D Civil War
8E London Old and New
Working with Texts 10 The Industrial Revolution
10D We the people
Final task: students write their own constitutions and display them on the wall.

Sport

2A P.E., I.C.T. and R.E.
Chill Zone 2 Swot Spot and Explode the Myth
3A Holiday Time
7C The Olympics
Chill Zone 5 Incredible but True
5C Goal
Final task: students make a poster about their favourite sport or about a sport from the ESW.

Natural history & endangered species

1E Tarantula
Chill Zone 1 Marmot
3D Local Festivals
5E Evolution
Chill Zone 5 Swot Spot
Profile on... India: page 154
Final task: students research an animal in terms of habitat, appearance and characteristics.

Civil rights

9E Slaves and Prospectors
8D "I have a dream..."
CD ROM 2, section D, (printable text) Rosa Parks and segregation
Final task: Chill zone 8 Organize your own campaign

Reading and Summary Skills

Some teachers will prefer to use a culture studies book to work on developing reading and summary skills with a view to preparing students for state examinations. There are ten long texts within the book and a further twenty-five for printing out from the CD Rom. The texts progress in conceptual and language difficulty through the book. All texts have pre-reading activities, comprehension questions and skills development activities to help students grasp summarizing concepts such as keyword selection, extracting the main points, paraphrasing, connecting ideas, transferring information correctly and using non-verbal clues. Besides the longer texts, reading skills on shorter texts are covered comprehensively in Crossing Cultures. Units with particular emphasis on developing reading skills include 1D, 2B, 2D, 2E, 3B, 3C, 3D, 4B, 5B, 5D, 5E, 6D, 6E, 7A, 7B, 7C, 7D, 7E, 8D, 9B, 9D, 10B, 10D.

Audio CD ROMs

The audio part of the CDs contains the listening activities which are integrated into the lessons. The CD Rom part of the 2 discs contains the following activities for use either in class or as homework:

- short texts with Cambridge ESOL KET-style multiple choice gapped text and true / false or multiple choice activities
- supplementary longer texts with comprehension questions and summary activities for students to print out

Crossing Cultures - TABLE OF CONTENTS

	BLOCK 1	BLOCK 2	BLOCK 3	BLOCK 4	BLOCK 5
A **SCHOOL LIFE AND EDUCATION**	pp. 8-9 **Going to School** Unusual ways children go to school Links: *Maths*	pp. 22-23 **P.E., I.C.T. and R.E.** School subjects Links: *P.E.*	pp. 36-37 **Holiday Time** School holidays and camp Links: *Literacy*	pp. 50-51 **2B or not 2B?** Classes, years and forms Links: *Maths and Science*	pp. 64-65 **What's Cool in School?** School fashion and school rules Links: *Citizenship*
B **PEOPLE AND LIFESTYLES**	pp. 10-11 **Chores, Chores, Chores!** Jobs children do at home Links: *Citizenship*	pp. 24-25 **Food, Glorious Food!** Food and drink Links: *Citizenship*	pp. 38-39 **My Room** Bedroom and bathroom culture Links: *Art and Design*	pp. 52-53 **Saturday Jobs** Kids who work Links: *Citizenship*	pp. 66-67 **Tea Time** Family mealtimes Links: *Citizenship*
C **SPORT & LEISURE**	pp. 12-13 **Join our Club** After school clubs Links: *Art and Design*	pp. 26-27 **What's on the Box?** Television Links: *Geography and Maths*	pp. 40-41 **Hanging out at the Mall** Shopping Links: *Maths*	pp. 54-55 **Read all about it!** Magazines and newspapers Links: *Media studies*	pp. 68-69 **Goal!** Sport in the ESW Links: *P.E.*
D **HISTORY AND TRADITIONS**	pp. 14-15 **Trick or Treat?** Autumn and winter festivals Links: *History*	pp. 28-29 **Touch Wood!** Superstitions and traditions Links: *History*	pp 42-43 **Local Festivals** Unusual local festivals in the ESW Links: *History*	pp. 56-57 **The Origins of English** The history of the language Links: *History*	pp. 70-71 **Pancake Day** Spring and summer festivals Links: *History*
E **THE WORLD WE LIVE IN**	pp. 16-17 **Tarantula!** Flora and fauna Links: *Science*	pp.30-31 **Extreme Weather** Weather disasters Links: *Science*	pp. 44-45 **Natural Wonders** Wonders of the natural world Links: *Science*	pp. 58-59 **Unsolved Mysteries** Places with legends and mysteries Links: *Science*	pp. 72-73 **Evolution** Darwin and the environment Links: *Science*
THE CHILL ZONE	pp. 18-19 **The Chill Zone 1**	pp. 32-33 **The Chill Zone 2**	pp. 46-47 **The Chill Zone 3**	pp. 60-61 **The Chill Zone 4**	pp. 74-75 **The Chill Zone 5**
WORKING WITH TEXTS	pp. 20-21 **Christmas in the ESW**	pp. 34-35 **Street Food: Past and Present**	pp. 48-49 **National Parks in Danger**	pp. 62-63 **Stonehenge - Who built it? What's it for?**	pp. 76-77 **Proms and Homecoming**

BLOCK 6	BLOCK 7	BLOCK 8	BLOCK 9	BLOCK 10	PROFILE ON...
pp. 78-79 **What did you get? I got a B** School reports and grades Links: *History*	pp. 92-93 **Public Schools** Types of schools Links: *Literature*	pp 106-107 **Home Education** Unusual education Links: *Science*	pp. 120-121 **My English Class** Learning English around the world Links: *Modern Languages*	pp. 134-135 **The New York Fame School** Getting home from school in New York Links: *Geography*	pp. 148-149 **AUSTRALIA and NEW ZEALAND** Focus on... Zoology
pp. 80-81 **Home Sweet Home** Types of homes Links: *Maths*	pp. 94-95 **Life Then and Life Now** Daily life in the past and today Links: *Design and Technology*	pp. 108-109 **Town and Country** Village, small town and city life Links: *Geography and Maths*	pp. 122-123 **ESW Religions** Religion and worship Links: *R.E.*	pp. 136-137 **Culture within a Culture** The Amish and Native Americans Links: *History and Science*	pp. 150-151 **CANADA** Focus on... Geography
pp. 82-83 **It's just a Craze** Crazes through the ages Links: *History*	pp. 96-97 **Going for Gold!** Sporting heroes Links: *P.E.*	pp. 110-111 **It Won 8 Oscars!** Cinema Links: *Media studies*	pp. 124-125 **Fashion** What's cool and what's not cool Links: *Citizenship*	pp. 138-139 **Music** From bebop to hip hop Links: *Music*	pp. 152-153 **THE COMMONWEALTH** Focus on... Cooperation
pp. 84-85 **Starting a New life** Immigration in the age of the steamship Links: *History*	pp. 98-99 **The Age of Discovery** 1492 and beyond Links: *History and Geography*	pp. 112-113 **"I have a dream…"** Civil and human rights Links: *Citizenship and History*	pp. 126-127 **Civil War!** The English and American civil wars Links: *History*	pp. 140-141 **"We the people…"** Constitutions and political systems Links: *History and Politics*	pp. 154-155 **INDIA** Focus on... Endangered Species
pp. 86-87 **One Small Step** Exploration: sea, land and space Links: *Science and Technology*	pp. 100-101 **Great Buildings** Manmade wonders and manmade mistakes Links: *Architecture*	pp. 114-115 **London Old and New** Dickens' London and London today Links: *History and Literature*	pp. 128-129 **Slaves and Prospectors** Cotton and gold in the USA Links: *Science and History*	pp. 142-143 **Inventors and Inventions** Famous English-speaking inventors Links: *Design and Technology*	pp. 156-157 **IRELAND** Focus on... Archaeology
pp. 88-89 **The Chill Zone 6**	pp. 102-103 **The Chill Zone 7**	pp. 116-117 **The Chill Zone 8**	pp. 130-131 **The Chill Zone 9**	pp. 144-145 **The Chill Zone 10**	pp. 158-159 **THE UK** Focus on... Meteorology
pp. 90-91 **Entering the New World**	pp. 104-105 **In and around London**	pp. 118-119 **Universal Studios Tour**	pp. 132-133 **The Pilgrim Fathers and the Mayflower**	pp. 146-147 **The Industrial Revolution**	pp 160-161 **THE USA** Focus on... Geology

GLOSSARY

pp. 162-168

SCHOOL LIFE AND EDUCATION **LESSON 1A**

Going to school — Unusual ways children go to school   pp. 8-9

This lesson introduces different methods of transport used by children to get to school.

Objectives: students will...	• learn / revise the lexis of methods of transport • learn about unusual ways some children in the ESW go to school • learn about the mile and learn the maths needed to convert to and from kilometres • read a pie chart with information about transport • complete a class survey
Warm-up	Students work in pairs to brainstorm a list of means of transport. Students may wish to use the photos on this page for inspiration. They include: a snowmobile; a boat; a school bus; a cable car; a post bus and a car.
1A CD1 Track 2	Students read and listen to match the speech bubbles to the photos. For **audio script** see Student's Book page 8. (**Accents:** 1. USA, 2. USA, 3. Eng, 4. Carib, 5. Scot, 6. Can.) **Culture note:** the post bus is a service offered by the Royal Mail. The population of some Scottish islands is so small that the postal service also doubles as a bus service. Key: 1. *E*, 2. *F*, 3. *A*, 4. *D*, 5. *B*, 6. *C*.
1B	Students answer the comprehension check questions. Key: 1. Who goes to school with their parents? *Chloe & Nat; Lucy.* 2. How many people go to school by road? *5: Kelly; Chloe & Nat; Dan & Jane.* 3. Who uses different transport in the winter and in the summer? *Travis.*
1C	Students use the words in the text to complete the sentences. This provides a model for talking about the ways they get to school. Key: A. Chloe and Nat go to school by *car*. B. Lucy's *Dad* takes her to school. C. Dan and Jane get the *post bus* to their school.
YOUR TURN	Students compare the ways they get to school.
2	Students use the conversion sum to calculate distances in miles and kilometres. Key: Dan and Jane live *32 km* from school.
3	Students answer a True / False quiz to find out how much they know about the mile. Key: 1. Australia, Canada, the USA, Britain and Ireland all use the mile. *True.* 2. There are 9 km in a mile. *False (there are 1.6 km in a mile).* 3. The mile is different from the nautical mile. *True (the nautical mile is 1.16 miles, 1.85 km).* 4. Mph means MP3 player. *False (it means miles per hour).*
4	The information in this activity comes from the UK government's statistical department. Students read the information in the pie chart and answer the questions. Key: 1. 27% of students go to school *by car.* 2. Only 1% of students go to school *by train.* 3. Most students in Britain go to school *on foot.* 4. 1/5 of all students go to school *by bus.*
OVER TO YOU	Students do a class survey of the ways they come to school. They present this information as a pie chart.
Optional Extension	Students design a form for use when doing a traffic survey with types of transport. They then complete the survey and draw a graph showing how many vehicles of what type pass every 10 minutes.
Optional Nip and Tuck	Students draw the transport survey pie chart at home.
Homework Option	Students write about their favourite means of transport. They illustrate their work with pictures cut from magazines or newspapers.
Web links	www.romans-in-britain.org.uk This site contains information about many aspects of the Roman legacy in Britain, including measurement. www.postbus.royalmail.com Information about the use of Royal Mail vehicles as public transport, including their use for tourists in remote areas. www.statistics.gov.uk This is an official UK government site. It contains statistics related to very many aspects of life in the UK including schools, transport etc.

PEOPLE AND LIFESTYLES   LESSON 1B

Chores, Chores, Chores!   Jobs children do at home   pp. 10-11

This lesson is concerned with chores and jobs children are expected to do at home. In the USA, most families have formalized chores. It is normal for children to do light housework from an early age. In the UK, this varies from family to family, but most children are expected to help with the running of the house.

Objectives: students will...	• learn / revise the lexis of household tasks • listen to young people from various countries in the ESW talking about their chores • do a quiz to assess how much or how little they help at home • discuss the contribution they make at home • revise adverbs of frequency • solve a maths problem
Warm-up CD1 Track 3	Give the students a few moments to look at the pictures. Play the track. Students tick the pictures of the chores they hear. **Key:** 1. *someone washing the car*; 2. *lawnmower*; 3. *someone laying the table*.
1	Students match the pictures with the list of chores. **Key:** 1. *G*, 2. *H*, 3. *F*, 4. *C*, 5. *E*, 6. *D*, 7. *A*, 8. *B*.
2 CD1 Track 4	Give students a few moments to read the list of chores. Check for comprehension difficulties. Play the track, pausing after each person. Students tick the chores the speakers do. Students should listen to the track twice, as happens in international examinations. They may need to listen more than twice in this instance. **Note:** Nick does no chores at all. **Culture note:** this activity is based on authentic interviews with teenagers. **Language note:** Nick says he is a 'couch potato'. This expression means "to sit on the sofa all day watching the TV". **Key:**

Chores	G	J	N	K
Wash the dog	✓			✓
Clean the windows				✓
Feed the fish		✓		
Make breakfast	✓			
Babysit				✓
Walk the dog		✓		
Make the bed	✓	✓		✓
Lay the table		✓		
Cut the grass	✓			
Wash the car	✓			
Clean the bathroom		✓		✓
Do the ironing	✓			
Take out the rubbish		✓		

Audio script
(**Accents:** Gary = USA, Jamaal = S. Eng, Katie = Aus, Nick = N. Eng.)

GARY   I wash the car and I wash the dog. I cut the grass in summer. I sometimes make breakfast and I always make my bed. I do my ironing.

JAMAAL   I make my bed and take out the rubbish. I walk the dog and I feed the fish. I sometimes clean the bathroom. I always lay the table.

NICK   I don't do any chores. My Mum does everything. I'm a couch potato!

KATIE   I wash the dog and I clean the windows. Um, sometimes I babysit my brother. I make the beds and I clean the bathroom.

YOUR TURN	Students have the opportunity to discuss the speakers' chores and workloads.
3	Show the meaning of couch potato with the Simpsons illustration. (**Language note** in exercise 2 above) Students do the quiz and add up their scores (**Key:** at the bottom of the page in the Student's Book). Allow students to compare their answers.
4	Students read the text and choose the correct alternative. **Key:** 1. *school*, 2. *Easter*, 3. *like*, 4. *cleaning*.
Did you know?	**Key:** 31·198 shoes per minute. This is also 7·799 shoes per person per minute.
OVER TO YOU	Students do web research in class or at home.
Optional Extensions	• Class survey of household chores. Students can then make a bar chart or a pie chart to illustrate the results. • Students write their own quiz on a different topic using adverbs of frequency. Topics could include what people do on Sundays, sports activities etc.
Homework Option	Ask students to keep a diary of their chores for a week. They can then compare their diaries with each other.
Web links	www.youthonline.ca Here you can find out about the types of chores Canadian children do and at what ages they are expected to do them.

SPORT & LEISURE LESSON **1C**

Join our club — After school clubs
pp. 12-13

This lesson introduces different types of clubs and associations which are popular in the English-speaking world. Some are traditional others are less so.

Objectives: students will...	• learn / revise the lexis of free-time activities • listen for specific information	• discuss and compare their own abilities and skills • design a poster for a club
Warm-up	Ask the class what clubs they belong to. Build up a list on the board. **Alternative warm-up:** What clubs are there where you live? Build up a list of clubs students could join locally.	
1	Students read the short text. They correct the sentences each of which contains one factual error. **Key:** 38 million young people in the world are scouts (*28 million*). Scouts meet three times a week (*once a week*). With these activities can get money (*badges*). Scouts never go to camp (*sometimes*).	
2	Students look at the badges with captions and match them to the description of activities scouts do in order to earn the badge. **Key:** 1. *F*, 2. *D*, 3. *E*, 4. *A*, 5. *G*, 6. *H*, 7. *B*, 8. *C*. **Pronunciation note:** a) Students may have difficulty with word stress on the names of the badges. Build up a chart on the board with the main stress marked: | Camp <u>cook</u>	<u>Climb</u>er	Enter<u>tain</u>er	In<u>ter</u>preter
Mete<u>o</u>rologist	As<u>tron</u>omer	<u>Art</u>ist	Can<u>o</u>eist | b) Remind students that the 'b' in 'mb' combinations is often silent. | climb	/klaɪm/
climber	/ˈklaɪmə/
bomb	/bɒm/
comb	/kəʊm/		
YOUR TURN	Students discuss which activities they can do.	
3A 3B **CD1 Track 5**	Give students a few moments to read through the items in the table and check the meaning of new items. The illustrations will help. Students then tick the activities they can do and report back to the class. Students should listen to the track twice, as happens in international examinations. Check students' answers. **Key:** 		TOMMY	BARBARA
Juggling		
Trapeze	✓	
Handstands		
Trick cycling		
Walking on stilts	✓	
Plate spinning		
Acrobatics		✓
Clowning		✓
Make-up			 **Audio script** (Accents: Eng) BARBARA Hi Tommy, what badge are you doing? TOMMY Circus skills. BARBARA Me too! What skills are you doing? TOMMY I want to do juggling but I'm not very good, so I'm doing handstands and plate spinning! BARBARA Plate spinning? Is it difficult? TOMMY Really difficult, I break a lot of plates, but I like it. What skills are you doing? BARBARA I'm doing clowning, you know acting like a clown. And I'm doing make-up. They go together, I think. TOMMY Well, good luck! BARBARA You too!	
OVER TO YOU	Students choose a club from the list or one of their own. They then make a poster for the club. If time is short, students could do this at home.	
Optional Extensions	• Telephone role play. Student A telephones Student B asking for information about membership of a club (day, time, cost, location). Student B uses the information on the poster to answer the questions. • Students research other fan clubs on the Internet. They look for information about membership, number of branches and activities.	
Homework Option	Ask students to write a short dialogue so they can earn their "Entertainer" scout badge.	
Web links	www.scoutbase.org.uk All about scouting including what scouts need to do to earn different badges. www.manutd.com The official website for Manchester United.	

HISTORY AND TRADITIONS LESSON **1D**

Trick or Treat? Autumn and winter festivals

pp. 14-15

This lesson introduces the autumn and winter festivals of Halloween, Bonfire Night, Diwali and Thanksgiving. Halloween (31st October) is widely celebrated in the ESW. Bonfire Night (5th November) is limited to the UK. Diwali is celebrated in India and in Hindu and Sikh populations throughout the world. Thanksgiving is an American tradition.

Objectives: students will...	• Find out about the history of autumn and winter festivals • Read & listen to short texts to extract specific information • Compare ESW festivals with those from their own countries
Warm-up	Students discuss their favourite autumn and winter festivals. **Note:** Christmas is not mentioned in this lesson as it is dealt with in **Working with Texts 1**. **Culture note:** Epiphany is not generally celebrated in the ESW, although it is marked in religious services.
1	Students match the Halloween characters to the pictures. **Key:** *witch, ghost, skeleton, wizard, goblin.*
2	Students read the information in the texts. They then match the texts to the pictures. **Pronunciation note:** Celtic /ˈkeltɪk/; Samhain /saʊn; ˈsaʊɪn; ˈsæwɪn/ **Key:** 1. *C*, 2. *A*, 3. *B*.
YOUR TURN	Give the students the opportunity to discuss possible tricks to play. These could include: ringing the doorbell and saying "I'm Count Dracula", leaving a fake spider or insect outside the person's door or dressing up as a ghost to scare the person. **Culture note:** American children are taught not to be destructive with Halloween tricks.
3A	Students read the texts and complete the table. **Culture note:** The Celtic tradition of Samhain was probably also mixed with the Roman festival of the goddess Pomona. She was the goddess of fruit trees. Apples are still associated with Halloween today (toffee apples and games with apples). **Key:**

Festival	Where do people celebrate it?	What's the origin or history?	What happens?	When is it?
Bonfire Night	The UK	1605 Guy Fawkes' plot	Make a guy; have a bonfire; light fireworks; eat sausages, baked potatoes & toffee	5th November
Diwali	India	Hindu and Sikh festival	Have fireworks and sweets; clean the house; wear new clothes	October or November

3B CD1 Track 6	Students listen to the information about Thanksgiving and tick the correct answers. Students should listen to the track twice, as happens in international examinations. **Key:** *USA, Pilgrim Fathers, eat turkey and watch baseball, fourth Thursday in November.* **Audio script (Accent: Eng)** In America, Thanksgiving is the beginning of the holiday season. The Pilgrim Fathers started the tradition of Thanksgiving in 1621. This was to say 'thank you' for the first good harvest in their new land. Today, people visit their families, eat roast turkey and watch baseball. Thanksgiving is on the fourth Thursday in November.
OVER TO YOU	Students work in pairs to look at their Halloween celebrations and to discuss bonfires, candles, fireworks and food on special occasions.
Optional Extensions	• Write a menu for a special festival. • Do a short web project on Diwali or the Gunpowder Plot.
Homework Options	• Write about New Year's Eve in your country. • Look online for a recipe for toffee.
Web links	www.holidays.net/thanksgiving Information about thanksgiving including menus and activities. www.halloween.com Information about Halloween. www.bbc.co.uk/schools/religion Information about Diwali and other festivals.

THE WORLD WE LIVE IN

LESSON 1E

Tarantula! Flora and fauna

pp. 16-17

In this lesson, students meet some of the variety of plants and animals to be found in the ESW. It is also a chance for students to look at ESW countries and where they are in the world.

Objectives: students will...	• investigate the appearance and habitats of plants and animals found in different ESW countries • place the ESW countries in the correct geographical locations on the world map • learn / revise adjectives which can be used to describe plants and animals • talk about animals they like in terms of habitat and characteristics
Warm-up	Students write kangaroo in the correct place on the map. **Alternative warm-up:** Ask students to label the following places on the world map: The USA, California, New Zealand, Canada, Hawaii, India, Australia, the UK, the Caribbean.
1	Check that students understand the adjectives in the table. **Pronunciation note:** students may have problems with the pronunciation of the following: 	tiny	/ˈtaɪni/
weird	/wɪəd/
cute	/kjuːt/ | Students skim read the text and put the animals into the table under the adjectives. Answers may vary as they are subjective and may appear in the students' answers more than once. **Suggested key:** | enormous	smelly	tiny	dangerous
---	---	---	---
moose redwood tree	skunk	katipo	cobra katipo
fast	**weird**	**delicious**	**poisonous**
bobcat	kiwi galliwasp	pineapple	cobra katipo	
YOUR TURN	Students decide which animals are scary and which animals are cute.
2A 2B CD1 Track 7	Students guess where the animals come from. Then play the CD. Students listen and check their answers. For **audio script** see Student's Book page 17. (**Accent:** GB) **Key:** *Redwood tree – California (or USA); Koalas – Australia; Katipo – New Zealand; Bobcat – North America; Kiwi – New Zealand; Skunks – USA; Moose – Canada; Galliwasp – Caribbean; Pineapples – Hawaii; Cobra – India.*
3	Students write the names of the plants and animals on the map showing where they are found. Ask students to compare their work with their partner as a check. **Culture note:** moose are known as elk in Europe.
OVER TO YOU	Students discuss their favourite animals in terms of habitat, appearance and characteristics. Information in the reading / listening exercise will help them.
Optional Extensions	• Students use the texts as a starter for writing their own short text about a wild animal native to their country. • Students look at another animal native to one of the countries in the lesson. Australia or New Zealand are particularly suitable. See: **Focus on... Zoology** in the **Profile on** section, page 149.
Homework Option	Students research one of the animals from the lesson in greater detail.
Web links	www.landcareresearch.co.nz New Zealand's environmental research organization. www.kamcom.co.nz/kiwi/kiwifacts.htm More information about the kiwi. www.nps.gov/redw/trees.html Photos and statistics about redwood trees. www.gomoose.com More about moose.

THE CHILL ZONE ①

pp. 18-19

CD1 Track 8 For the woodchuck tongue twister **audio script** see Student's Book page 18. (**Accent:** USA)

Wordsearch
Key:

```
S S P R T U B E Q J
C N E F U R R I C A
A M O P E N U R K M
B O T W H R U X M E
L E T R A M N R O O M
E A R T H O U Y P F
C A M A D O B I E E
A P L N I M U I D R
R B I K A N R P L R
Y A E R O P L A N E
```

Extra word (upside down at the bottom of the page in the Student's Book): **aeroplane**

Experiment
For the experiment you will need: a fresh pineapple, a sharp knife, some compost and a flower pot.

Swot spot
Key: 1a. *by* 1b. *by* 1c. *on*, 2. *1.6 km in a mile*, 3. e.g. *The UK, the USA, Australia*.

CD1 Track 9 For the rhyme **audio script**, see Student's Book page 19. (**Accent:** Eng)

SPOT THE DIFFERENCE:
In **B** there are spots on the plate, the ringmaster hasn't got a tie, the trapeze artist hasn't got a scarf, the trick cyclist hasn't got a hat, the juggler has got four balls, the bicycle is yellow.

WORKING WITH TEXTS 1

pp. 20-21

Christmas in the ESW
This is the first long text in a section aimed at preparing students for state examinations. The texts are graded according to level and are progressive. Each text is followed by a series of comprehension questions and work on summary skills.

Culture note: "Christmas dinner" is the name of the special meal, although it can be eaten at lunchtime or in the evening without changing its name.

Before you read
1. Give the students the opportunity to brainstorm words associated with Christmas. Words in the text include: present / decoration / tree / holly / mistletoe / crib / card / reindeer / Santa Claus / Father Christmas / Saint Nicholas / Christmas Eve / chimney / stocking / carol / turkey / Christmas pudding / cracker / Boxing Day

Reading
2. Students read the text and answer the comprehension questions.
Key: 1. *The day after Thanksgiving*; 2. *With Christmas trees, holly, mistletoe, a crib and Christmas cards*; 3. *He goes down the chimney*; 4. *Children in every house leave food and drink for Santa*; 5. *To receive letters to Santa*; 6. *Songs or hymns*; 7. *Turkey / Christmas pudding*; 8. *A joke / little present / paper hat*; 9. *Barbecue*; 10. *26th December*.

Summary skills
3. As a first approach to summarizing, students fill the gaps in the sentences, using words from the text.
Key: *important / Christmas trees, holly, mistletoe and cards / stockings / letter / carols / dinner / families / go shopping*

SCHOOL LIFE AND EDUCATION   LESSON **2A**

P.E., I.C.T. and R.E. School subjects
pp. 22-23

This lesson introduces the various subjects secondary school students study at school.

Objectives: students will...	• learn / revise the lexis of school subjects • learn about unusual subjects studied in other countries • describe a typical school day • compare the length of school day in different countries • learn / revise the lexis of sports • discuss favourite sports
Warm-up	Students guess what P.E., I.C.T. and R.E. stand for and then discuss which of these subjects they like best. **Key:** *P.E. = Physical Education, I.C.T. = Information & Communication Technology, R.E. = Religious Education.*
1 YOUR TURN	Students look at the list of English secondary school subjects and tick the ones they study. Some of the subjects will be new to students and, in **Your Turn**, they should then discuss which they would like to introduce into their schools. **Culture note:** citizenship. This encompasses various aspects of community life such as human rights, the legal system, voting and democracy, the free press, voluntary groups and conflict resolution.
2A	Students complete the timetable with their typical Monday. **Tip:** alternative questions to use with a stronger group: Where do students start school the earliest? *The USA.* Where do students finish school the latest? *The UK.* Where do students have the most lessons? *The USA and the UK.* Where is the school day the longest? *The USA 7½ hours.* **Culture notes:** "I don't like Mondays" was a 1980s song by British rock group The Boomtown Rats. American school timetables vary from state to state. 'Maths' is the British English abbreviation for Mathematics; 'Math' is the American.
2B	Students finish the sentences. **Key:** The answers to this exercise depend on your own school timetable
2C	Students compare break times and lesson length **Key:** Are lessons always the same length? *Yes in the UK. No in the USA.* How long are the breaks in each country? *15 minutes UK. 30 minutes USA.*
YOUR TURN	Students decide which of the timetables they prefer.
3	Students look at the pictures of common sports in the UK and USA and answer the questions with the help of the photos. **Culture note:** there are differences between British and American English as far as sports are concerned. Hockey in the US is played on ice (UK ice hockey). Football in the US is different from soccer. Football is the usual name for soccer in the UK. Netball is a type of basketball and is usually played by girls. **Key:** 1. *All except for hockey (USA) which uses a puck;* 2. *Hockey (both) football (UK) & soccer, basketball and netball;* 3. *Hockey (USA);* 4. *Cricket, baseball, hockey (UK);* 5. *It's a contact sport in the US. The ball is oval;* 6. *Open question.*
4 CD1 Track 10	Give students a few moments to read through the questions. Students listen for the sports Karen plays and watches. Students should listen to the track twice, as happens in international examinations. Check students' answers. **Key:** Which sports does she play? *Hockey and netball.* Which sports does she watch? *Cricket and football.* **Language note:** 'on the box' this is a colloquial expression meaning 'on the television'. **Audio script** (Accent: Eng) I'm sports-mad. I like watching cricket in the summer, especially international test matches, but I never play. I really don't like watching American football – I don't understand it. In the winter, I play hockey and netball at school and I sometimes go to football matches, but I usually watch football on the box.
OVER TO YOU	Students work in pairs or small groups to ask and answer questions about sports.
Optional Extension	Students talk in pairs about sports. They discuss a sport in terms of number of players / championships / how to play.
Homework Option	Students collect photos of their favourite sports / players and glue them into their notebooks with information about the sport / player.
Web links	www.bbc.co.uk/wales/schoolgate/aboutschool/content/curriculumsecondary.shtml Information about the national curriculum. www.woodlands-junior.kent.sch.uk/customs/questions/education/secsch.htm A day in the life of a school student.

PEOPLE AND LIFESTYLES LESSON 2B

Food, Glorious Food! Food and drink pp. 24-25

This lesson introduces the concept of school dinners around the world and cultural differences in food from different countries. **Note:** school dinner is eaten at lunchtime.

Objectives: students will...	• learn / revise the lexis of food • talk about takeaway food • group food into categories • listen to people talking about school dinners • read a short newspaper article • discuss annoying habits
Warm-up	Students discuss their favourite foods. **Alternative warm-up:** lead a class brainstorm by writing different foods on the board divided into yellow, red and green foods.
1A	Students look at the photos of the different types of food and place them on the great / gross meter according to their tastes. **Culture note:** chips. In the UK these are strips of potato eaten hot (US French fries). In the US they are potato rounds sold in packets (UK crisps).
1B	Students vote on their favourite and least favourite foods.
2A	Students work in pairs to discuss which things from the table they have for lunch in order to prepare them for listening.
2B CD1 Track 11	Students listen to six students talking about their school dinners. Students should listen to the track twice, as happens in international examinations. Check students' answers. **Pronunciation note:** Yoghurt has 2 pronunciations: /ˈjəʊgət; jɒgət;/. Seamus /ˈʃeɪməs/ **Key:**

	chicken	chocolate	curry	sandwiches	fruit	rice	crisps	soup
Imran	✓					✓		
Chloe	✓				✓	✓		
Seamus		✓		✓	✓		✓	
Kelly				✓	✓		✓	
Will		✓		✓				✓
Jenny	✓		✓	✓				

Audio script (**Accents:** see Student's Book page 24)

IMRAN In India we usually have vegetables or chicken for lunch at school. We eat it with rice and sometimes we put yoghurt on top. I like the lunches.

CHLOE I live in Bridgetown, Barbados. Our school dinners are great. My favourite is chicken and rice and we always have some fruit.

SEAMUS We don't usually have school dinners in Ireland, so I bring a packed lunch to school. I often have sandwiches, chocolate and crisps. Sometimes I have some fruit as well.

KELLY In New Zealand, we usually bring packed lunches to school. Children usually have sandwiches, crisps and fruit. I prefer the idea of school lunches.

WILL Some kids in America have school lunches, but most bring their own packed lunch. I often bring soup and sandwiches. Sometimes I have a bar of chocolate as well.

JENNY Our school dinners are sometimes really good. My favourite is curry or chicken. Some schools have gross school dinners, so the kids bring sandwiches.

YOUR TURN	Students give opinions on the school dinners in the ESW
3A	Students predict the content of the reading text. This is also a vocabulary check.
3B	Students read the text. Check to see if student predictions match the text. **Language note:** 'to be sick of' = to be bored with or to be fed up with. 'To make a meal of something' = to make too much of a fuss about it.
3C	Students order the pictures according to the information in the text. **Key:** 1. A, 2. B, 3. F, 4. E, 5. D, 6. C.
OVER TO YOU	Students work in pairs to discuss annoying habits.
Optional Extension	Students design a menu for lunches at their school.
Homework Option	Students keep a food diary of all the things they eat during the week.
Web links	http://news.bbc.co.uk/cbbcnews Chat and news for young people about school. www.bbc.co.uk/food Britain's favourite food.

SPORT & LEISURE

LESSON 2C

What's on the Box? Television

pp. 26-27

This lesson introduces the concept of TV programme formats.

Objectives: students will...	• learn / revise the lexis of types of TV programmes • do a class survey • devise a bar chart to show TV programmes students watch	• listen to an interview and the excerpt from a TV Quiz Show • devise a quiz for other students
Warm-up	Lead a class discussion on TV habits. **Alternative warm-up:** question and answer session e.g. How many TVs have you got? Where do you usually watch TV?	
1A CD1 Track 12	Students read and listen to Robbie's interview and choose the correct answers. Students should listen to the track twice, as happens in international examinations. Check students' answers. **Language note:** 'Front room' is a common alternative to living room / lounge. **Key:** How many TVs are there in your house, Robbie? *Four*. What are your favourite types of programme? *Reality shows and quiz shows*. Where do you usually watch TV? *In the front room*. When do you usually watch TV? *In the evening*.	**Audio script** (**Accents:** GB and S. Eng.) INT. How many TVs are there in your house, Robbie? ROBBIE Oh, let me think. There's one in my room, one in the kitchen and one in my parents' room and one in the front room, so that's four. INT. And what are your favourite types of programme? ROBBIE Well I don't really like documentaries but docudramas are ok. What I really like are reality shows, you know, Big Brother and that kind of thing. I also like quiz shows. INT. Where do you usually watch TV? ROBBIE I sometimes watch it in my room, but I usually watch TV in the front room with my mum and dad. INT. When do you usually watch TV? ROBBIE I generally watch it in the evening after school. INT. OK, thanks very much!
1B	Students work in pairs to ask and answer the questions. Circulate to monitor responses.	
2A	Students read the information contained in the bar chart and answer the questions. **Key:** 1. *Quiz Shows*, 2. *27*, 3. *Food Programmes*, 4. *Docudramas* and *Sitcoms*.	
2B	Students do a class survey about TV-watching habits in the group. This could be a pairwork or a teacher-led activity, depending on time constraints. Students use the information to design their own bar chart.	
3A	Students guess the answers to the geography quiz questions about the ESW. **Culture note:** in question 4, all the answers relate to real mountains A = Ben Nevis, B = Mount Everest, C = Mont Blanc, D = The Matterhorn (Monte Cervino).	
3B CD1 Track 13	Students listen to the text and check their answers. Students should listen to the track twice, as happens in international examinations. Check students' answers. **Key:** 1. *A, Canberra*; 2. *C, Arizona*; 3. *C, New Zealand*; 4. *A, 1,343 m*. **Audio script** (**Accents:** Eng) QUIZMASTER Ok, are you ready? CONTESTANT Yes, go ahead. QUIZMASTER Ok. Question 1. What's the capital of Australia? Is it a) Canberra? b) Sydney? c) Auckland? d) Paris? CONTESTANT It's answer a) Canberra. QUIZMASTER Are you sure? CONTESTANT Yes, quite sure. QUIZMASTER That's the correct answer. Question 2: Where's the Grand Canyon? Is it a) in Florida? b) on the moon? c) in Arizona? or d) in Alaska? CONTESTANT Oh, um I think it's in Arizona, yes, it is. Answer c) Arizona. QUIZMASTER Ok, is that your final answer? CONTESTANT Yes, it's my final answer.	QUIZMASTER And that's right, well done. Question 3: Where do Maoris come from? Do they come from a) Germany? b) Ireland? c) New Zealand? or are they from d) Australia? CONTESTANT Oh that's answer c) New Zealand. I'm certain. QUIZMASTER Ok and that's correct, well done again. Question 4: The highest mountain in Great Britain is Ben Nevis, but how high is it? Is it a) 1,343 metres high? b) 8,848 metres high? c) 4,807 metres high? Or d) 4,477 metres high? CONTESTANT Ooooh, um that's really difficult. Is it d) 4,477 metres high? Um, yes, d). QUIZMASTER Oh, no I'm sorry. The answer is actually a) 1,343 metres high.
OVER TO YOU	Students work in pairs to prepare a quiz on geography for another pair, using the prompts on the page.	
Optional Extension	Students research another TV format (e.g. Big Brother or Fame Academy).	
Optional Nip and Tuck	The bar chart activity in 2B could be set as homework.	
Homework Option	Ask students to write a short dialogue so they can earn their "Entertainer" scout badge.	
Web links	www.bbc.co.uk The main website for the BBC. www.radiotimes.com A radio and TV listings magazine with schedules and articles about current programmes and TV personalities.	

HISTORY AND TRADITIONS

LESSON 2D

Touch Wood! Superstitions and traditions
pp. 28-29

This lesson explores the concepts of lucky and unlucky in the ESW.

Objectives: students will...	• learn / revise the lexis of lucky symbols • learn idiomatic expressions related to the topic • learn about the history of the Black Death • compare attitudes to superstition • discuss lucky and unlucky objects
Warm-up	Students discuss their lucky numbers and colours and any lucky charms they might have.
1	Students read the short texts and decide whether the items bring good or bad luck. **Key:** Bad luck: *a broken mirror, a white cat, one magpie, an "n"-shaped horseshoe.* Good luck: *a "u"- shaped horseshoe, black-eyed peas, a black cat, a four-leaf clover.*
YOUR TURN	Students compare attitudes from their own countries.
2A	Students read the dictionary definition of 'touch wood' and discuss how to express this in their own language.
2B CD1 Track 14	Students read the text and listen to the expressions. While reading and listening they should match the expressions with the pictures. Allow the students time to practise these expressions. **Tip:** encourage the students to use expressions such as 'bless you' and 'fingers crossed' when possible in class. For **audio script** see Student's Book page 28. (**Accent:** GB) **Key:** 1 = C, 2 = B, 3 = D, 4 = A.
3 CD1 Track 15	This activity picks up on the issue of magpies bringing good or bad luck. Students listen to the rhyme and fill the gaps. Students may need to listen twice as happens in international examinations. **Audio script and key** (**Accent:** GB) One for *sorrow* Two for *joy* Three for a *girl* Four for a *boy* Five for *silver* Six for *gold* Seven for a *secret* never to be told
4 CD1 Track 16	Reading comprehension related to the Black Death and the superstitions attached to it. Students read the text and then tick the True / False boxes. They listen to the rhyme. For **audio script** see Student's Book page 29. (**Accent:** Eng) **Key:** 1. *False* (a lot of rhymes come from historical events); 2. *True*; 3. *True*; 4. *False* (the ring o' roses referred to the rash); 5. *True*; 6. *True*.
OVER TO YOU	Students discuss superstitions and traditions in their own countries.
Optional Extension	Project on the Black Death or another infectious disease relevant to the history of the country e.g. malaria, cholera.
Homework Option	Students research another nursery rhyme on the internet.
Web links	http://nurseryrhymes.allinfoabout.com The history of nursery rhymes. www.biologycorner.com/quests/outbreak Acting out an epidemic. www.corsinet.com/trivia Unusual superstitions. www.irishcultureandcustoms.com All about customs and traditions in Ireland.

THE WORLD WE LIVE IN

LESSON 2E

Extreme Weather   Weather disasters

pp. 30-31

This lesson addresses some of the more extreme weather conditions which are found in some areas of the ESW.

Objectives: students will...	• learn / revise adjectives used to describe weather conditions • learn / revise superlatives of these common adjectives • learn about tornadoes and hurricanes • do a tornado experiment • discuss disaster response and what to do in an emergency
Warm-up	Students discuss today's weather.
1A	Students match the adjectives with the superlative form. **Key:** 1. *E*, 2. *C*, 3. *F*, 4. *D*, 5. *A*, 6. *B*. **Pronunciation note:** many students will need reinforcement of the pronunciation of the following: | strongest | /ˈstrɒŋɡəst/ | | largest | /ˈlɑːdʒəst/ |
1B	Students fill the gaps in the text using the superlatives. **Key:** *wettest, sunniest, strongest, thickest, largest, coldest.*
1C CD1 Track 17	**Audio script and key** (**Accent:** Eng) The *wettest* place in the world is Cherrapunji in India. It usually has 1,270 cm of rain in a year. This is because of monsoons. The *sunniest* place in the world is Yuma in Arizona, USA. It has 4,055 hours of sunshine a year. The maximum possible is 4,456 hours! The *strongest* wind ever recorded was 371 km/h. This was in New Hampshire, USA, in April 1934. The *thickest* fogs happened in London in the 1950s. They were smogs (**sm**oke and **fog**) and many people died. Today they don't happen because of pollution controls. The *largest* hailstone fell in Kansas, USA in 1970. It was 43 cm in circumference and weighed 1 kg. The *coldest* place in the world is the Antarctic. Its lowest ever temperature was -89.4 °C. In some places the ice is 4.8 km thick.
2	Students extract the main information from the texts to complete the table about tornadoes and hurricanes. **Culture note:** In the film *The Wizard of Oz*, Dorothy is swept up by a tornado. **Key:** | | **Hurricane** | **Tornado** | | --- | --- | --- | | force measure | Category 1 - 5 | Torro Scale | | alternative names | cyclones / typhoons | twisters | | disaster dates | (Katrina) August 2005 | April 3rd 1974 | | wind speed | 120 km/h | 500 km/h | | famous films | Hurricane Andrew | Twister / Night of the Twisters |
3	Experiment. Students can do this at home if classroom conditions are not suitable. **You will need:** two empty plastic water bottles, glue, a sharp object for making a hole, water. **See illustrations** in the Student's Book page 31 for how to proceed.
OVER TO YOU	Students work in pairs to make a list of things people need after natural disasters.
Optional Extensions	• If your country is prone to disasters such as earthquakes and flooding, students could work to produce guidelines for an emergency such as what to do, what not to do. • **Photocopiable worksheet** on page 76 of this Teacher's Book. Students observe the weather for a week and work out average temperature and average rainfall.
Homework Option	Students keep a weather diary for a week and note down the weather conditions daily.
Web links	www.bom.gov.au Australian weather facts and figures. www.metoffice.gov.uk Weather forecast in English.

THE CHILL ZONE 2

pp. 32-33

FOODWORD
Key:
Across: 2. *crisps*; 5. *chocolate*; 7. *fruit*; 8. *cabbage*.
Down: 1. *sprouts*; 3. *milk*; 4. *ice-cream*; 5. *curry*; 6. *liver*; 9. *blue*.

Song: "Raining in my heart"

CD1 Track 18 Audio script and key:

The *sun* is out	The weatherman
The *sky* is blue	Says *fine* today
There's not a *cloud*	He doesn't know
To spoil the view	You've gone away
But it's *raining*	And it's *raining*
Raining in my heart.	*Raining* in my heart.

The song is repeated twice and the final 2 lines are repeated to fade.

WORKING WITH TEXTS 2

pp. 34-35

Street Food: Past and Present

This is the second long text in a section aimed at preparing students for state examinations. The texts are graded according to level and are progressive. Each text is followed by a series of comprehension questions and work on summary skills.

Before you read
1 Give the students the opportunity to brainstorm words associated with international food. These could include *Chinese food, curries, kebabs, Middle-Eastern cooking, Greek food* etc.

Reading
2 Students read the text and answer the questions.
Key:
1. *In the streets*; 2. *Bread and olives*; 3. *Belgium = waffles, France = crêpes*; 4. *Roti comes from Trinidad and Tobago and is a type of flat bread*; 5. *In India*; 6. *In Canada*; 7. *Hot dog*; 8. *Chinese, Caribbean, Mexican, Vietnamese, Thai and Indian food, pizza and ice-cream*; 9. *High quantities of fat, sugar and salt*; 10. *Sugar and salt content*.

Summary skills
3 This activity works on using connectors to make texts more cohesive. Students are presented with a summary and fill the gaps with connectors.
Key:
and / because / and / because / so

23

SCHOOL LIFE AND EDUCATION

LESSON 3A

Holiday Time — School holidays and camp
pp. 36-37

This lesson explores school holidays and summer holiday activities in the English-speaking world. The summer camp activities are a composite of several real summer camps in the USA.

Objectives: students will...	• learn / revise the lexis of school landmark days • learn / revise the lexis of free-time activities • learn about summer camp in the USA • compare times and lengths of school holidays • write a short letter
Warm-up	Students discuss their next holiday and how long it lasts.
1A	Students look at the dates on the calendar and answer the questions about the USA. **Culture note:** the dates from the USA vary from state to state. **Key:** The school year starts on *September 4th*. The school year ends on *June 8th*.
1B	Students mark the public holidays on the calendar. **Culture note:** Memorial Day is a day of remembrance for those who have died in service of the USA. It is the last Monday in May. Veterans Day is celebrated on 11th November (or the nearest weekday) the same day as Armistice Day or Remembrance Day in other parts of the world. The aim is to acknowledge the contribution of living veterans of the United States Armed Services. **Key:** the dates are as follows: Martin Luther King Day = *Jan 15th*, President's Day = *Feb 19th*, Memorial Day = *May 28th*, Columbus Day = *Oct 9th*, Veterans Day = *Nov 11th*, Thanksgiving = *Nov 23rd*. **Punctuation note:** "Veterans Day" is written without an apostrophe.
1C CD1 Track 19	Give students a few moments to read through the text. Students listen for dates of holidays in the UK. Students should listen to the track twice, as happens in international examinations. Check students' answers. **Audio script and key** (Accent: Eng) Well this year we start on September the *1st*, which is a Friday. Then we have our half term break from October the *23rd* to the *29th*. We break up for Christmas on the *19th* and we go back to school again on January the *3rd*. Half term in the Spring term is from Feb the *19th* till the *25th*, then the Easter break is from the *2nd* of April till the *15th*. We get extra day off in May for the May Day Bank Holiday, that's on the *7th* and then we have half term again from the *28th* of May till June the *3rd*. We break up on July the *20th*. **Language note:** in spoken British English we usually say 'the' and 'of' when giving a date. These are not usually written.
1D	Students write the UK holiday dates on the calendar. They should use a different colour so they can compare all the holidays at a later stage.
YOUR TURN	Students write their own holiday dates on the calendar and then count up the days so that they can compare the USA, the UK and their own country in terms of holiday length.
2	Students look at the timetable of activities and answer the True / False questions. **Note:** the blanks on the camp timetable are for students to complete in exercise 3. Point out the list of forbidden items. **Culture note:** it is very common for American kids to go to summer camp at some point during their school vacation. There are many different types of camp, but most integrate sports and team-building activities into their camp activities. **Language note:** R & R stands for rest and relaxation. Cell phone is AmE, mobile phone is BrE. **Key:** 1. *False* (jogging is optional), 2. *True*, 3. *False*, 4. *True*.
3	Students choose 2 morning and 2 afternoon activities they would like to do and add them into the timetable. Allow class discussion about the type of activities students like to do.
OVER TO YOU	Students write a letter home. This is the type of writing activity students are expected to do for the KET examination from Cambridge ESOL.
Optional Extension	Students could design a programme for Christmas / Easter or Summer camp activities, depending on the time of year you are using this unit.
Homework Option	Students make a list of activities they would like to learn in the future, using the template in exercise 3.
Web links	www.kidscamps.com For information about types of camp. www.campamerica.co.uk For people who want to work in camp. www.mountainmeadow.com An example of a typical summer camp.

PEOPLE AND LIFESTYLES   LESSON **3B**

My Room — Bedroom and bathroom culture   pp. 38-39

This lesson introduces the subject of kids' own space in the UK and USA. It also allows students to compare cultural differences.

Objectives: students will...	• learn / revise the lexis of free-time activities • learn / revise the lexis of bedroom and bathroom furniture • learn about different habits in different areas of the world • compare their own lifestyles with those of others • redesign their rooms
Warm-up	Students talk about what they have on the walls of their rooms.
1A	Students read the texts and match them with the photos. **Key:** 1. *B*, 2. *D*, 3. *A*, 4. *C*.
1B CD1 Track 20	Students listen to Rachel and tick the activities she likes doing in her room. Students should listen to the track twice, as happens in international examinations. Check students' answers. **Audio script and key** (Accent: Eng) I really like my room – it's my personal space. I like *doing my homework* in my room because it's quiet and I can concentrate. I like *watching TV* as well, because I can choose my programmes and don't have a problem with my brother. I like *reading* and *texting my friends*. Sometimes we *have sleepovers* – that's great fun. I can't surf the net. I don't have a computer in my bedroom.
YOUR TURN	Students make a list of activities they prefer to do in their rooms.
2	Students tick statements that are true about their homes. **Note:** this introduces concepts which are important for students who travel, such as tolerance and the expectation that things will be different in different countries. Students read the texts about Anna, Marc and Francesca who are all studying overseas. They complete the table for each country. **Key:** |	Australia	USA	Scotland
---	---	---	---
There are posters on the bedroom walls.		✓	
There is carpet in the bathroom.		✓	
There is carpet in the kitchen.			✓
There are two taps on the washbasin: one for cold water, one for hot.			✓
There isn't a bidet in the bathroom.	✓	✓	✓
There is a swimming pool.	✓		
There is a barbecue area.	✓		
There are telephones in all the bedrooms.		✓	
Baths and toilets are in different rooms.			✓	
OVER TO YOU	Students draw a plan of their rooms in their notebooks and place the normal bedroom furniture in it. They then add three luxury items of their choice and compare with a partner.
Optional Extension	Student could discuss the things they like and the things they don't like about their houses.
Homework Option	Students make notes from TV programmes about things which are different in American homes.
Web links	www.biltmore.com Facts about the largest family home in the world. www.yha.org.uk Information about cultural differences and youth hostels.

25

SPORT & LEISURE LESSON **3C**

Hanging out at the Mall — Shopping

pp. 40-41

This lesson introduces the concept of shopping.

Objectives: students will...	• learn / revise the lexis of types of shops • learn / revise the lexis of shopping • learn about cultural differences related to shopping in the UK	• do a maths problem related to a shopping budget • discuss what they would like to buy
Warm-up	Discussion on shopping and purchases.	
1A	Students read the information about the Trafford Centre for specific information and complete the table. **Key:** | THE TRAFFORD CENTRE	
---	---
Number of shops	300
Types of shops	clothes shop, department store, bookshop, newsagent, bank, shoe shop, music shop, toy shop, gift shop.
Number of restaurants	36
Car parking space	10,000 cars
Number of shoppers every year	30 million people
Opening hours	10 am – 10 pm, every day
Number of workers	6,000		
1B	Students discuss shopping centres in their town on the basis of the categories in the table.	
2	Students discuss the type of shop by using the clues from the signs. Students should draw a table in their notebooks. **Tip:** with weaker groups, give the headings: cafés and restaurants, clothes shops, shoe shops and toy shops. **Key:** Pizza Eater, The Coffee Shop, Pete's Diner, The All Day Breakfast Joint, Giovanni's Ices are *cafés and restaurants*. The Sock Box, Kidz Clothes, The Scottish Jumper Shop, The Tracksuit are *clothes shops*. Boots and Braces, Sally's Sandals, The Trainer Shop are *shoe shops*. Supertoys, Games Galore are *toy shops*.	
3A CD1 Track 21	Give students a few moments to read through the items. Students listen for the locations Gavin visits on his shopping trip. Students should listen to the track twice, as happens in international examinations. Check students' answers. **Key:** café, clothes shop. **Audio script (Accents: Eng)** Conversation 1 WAITER ... and for you? GAVIN I'll have a cappuccino and er… a roast beef sandwich please. WAITER Brown or white? GAVIN White bread please. WAITER Anything else? GAVIN No that's all thanks. Conversation 2 SHOP ASST. Can I help you? GAVIN Er... Yes. Erm... Have you got these trousers in a smaller size? SHOP ASST. Just a minute. Let me check…Yes, but we've only got them in grey not black. GAVIN No, I really wanted black. Thanks anyway. SHOP ASST. Thank you. GAVIN Bye. SHOP ASST. Bye.	
3B	This is a maths exercise. Students read the text and calculate how much money Gavin has left over at the end of his shopping trip. **Key:** £2.44	
OVER TO YOU	Students decide what they would buy with £35 and compare.	
Shopping tips in the UK	Focus on the differences between shopping in the UK and in your country. **Culture note:** showing two fingers in this way is an offensive gesture in the UK.	
Optional Extension	Students could plan a shopping centre or work on the names of shops with a floor plan of their local shopping centre.	
Homework Option	Students write about their last shopping trip and what they bought.	
Web link	www.westedmall.com The world's largest shopping centre. www.traffordcentre.co.uk One of Britain's biggest shopping centres.	

26

HISTORY AND TRADITIONS
LESSON 3D

Local Festivals
Unusual local festivals in the English-speaking world pp. 42-43

This lesson continues the theme of festivals, but this time introducing some local ones in contrast to the better known national celebrations.

Objectives: students will...	• learn / revise the lexis of local festivals • find out about the origins of funfairs • match headlines to texts • extract specific information from a text • do a Cambridge ESOL KET-style speaking activity
Warm-up	Students discuss funfairs and when they come to their town.
1A CD1 Track 22	**Pronunciation note:** Punxsutawney /ˈpʌŋksəˌtɔːni/ Look through the headlines with the students. Use the picture to illustrate what a groundhog looks like. Students read and listen to the text and match the headlines to the articles. There are six headlines, but only three are needed. For **audio script** see Student's Book page 42. (**Accent:** GB) **Key:** Text 1: *What is Groundhog Day?*, Text 2: *European Origins*, Text 3: *Things to do on Groundhog Day*.
1B	Students read the texts about Mop Fairs and Rodeos and complete the table. **Key:**

	What is it?	What is the origin?	What do people do?
Mop Fair	funfair	Medieval job fair	go on rides, watch parades, go to the market, have a pig roast
Rodeo	horse-riding and cowboy festival	Spanish origin	go to the funfair, watch cowboy competitions, ride horses, watch pig races

OVER TO YOU	This is a KET-style speaking activity. Students work in pairs. One student uses the prompts to ask questions, the other uses the information on the poster to answer the questions. Students swap roles.
Optional Extension	Students write a short article about a local festival. If they come from different areas of the city or different towns and villages, you could make a class display of local festivals and traditions.
Homework Option	Students design a poster about their local festival. They should use the poster about Stoking Castle as a guide.
Web links	www.bbc.co.uk/coventry/features/stories/2002/09/all-the-fun-of-the-fair.shtml The history of mop fairs presented as a news article. www.rodeohouston.com The Houston rodeo website with a downloadable brochure of activities. www.groundhog.org All about Punxsutawney Phil with games and quizzes for students to do.

THE WORLD WE LIVE IN

LESSON 3E

Natural Wonders — Wonders of the natural world — pp. 44-45

This lesson introduces a selection of the most famous natural wonders in the ESW. Students also learn about the formation of these wonders and the effects of erosion on the landscape and the world around us.

Objectives: students will...	• learn / revise the lexis of some geographical features • learn / revise the lexis of erosion • learn about how natural wonders are formed • plan a trip to the Grand Canyon • discuss erosion in the world around them
Warm-up CD1 Track 23	Students listen to the place names and guess where they are (**Audio script part 1**). Students listen again to check their answers (**Audio script part 2**). **Key:** Giant's Causeway: *Northern Ireland*; Old Faithful: *Yellowstone National Park, USA*; The Great Barrier Reef: *Australia;* Uluru (formerly known as Ayers Rock), *Australia*; Grand Canyon: *Arizona, USA*. **Audio script part 1** (Accent: Eng) Giant's Causeway / Old Faithful / The Grand Canyon / Uluru / The Great Barrier Reef **Audio script part 2** (Accent: Eng) Giant's Causeway is in Ireland. Old Faithful is in Yellowstone National Park in the USA. The Great Barrier Reef is in Australia. Uluru is in Australia. The Grand Canyon is in Arizona in the United States.
YOUR TURN	Students discuss any other natural wonders they know. Examples could be volcanos such as Etna or Vesuvius, mountains such as Mont Blanc or Everest, seas such as the Dead Sea.
1A	Students read the information about the formation of natural wonders. They then guess how each of the five natural wonders was formed. **Tip:** encourage students to look at the pictures to help them decide.
1B CD1 Track 24	Listen to the track so that students can check whether their guesses were right. **Pronunciation note:** geyser BrE /ˈgiːzə/; AmE /ˈgaɪzər/ **Audio script and key** (Accent: Eng) The Grand Canyon is one of the world's greatest natural wonders. It was formed millions of years ago mainly *by water erosion* from the Colorado River. Uluru is one of Australia's most famous natural wonders. Its old name was Ayers Rock. It is a mountain and it was formed *by water erosion and wind erosion*. The Great Barrier Reef is also in Australia. It is the largest coral reef in the world. It was formed *by living organisms* called coral over thousands of years. Giant's Causeway is in Northern Ireland. It is made of lava and was formed *by volcanic activity* and fast cooling. Old Faithful is in Yellowstone Park in the United States. It is a geyser. It explodes every 80 minutes because of *volcanic activity*.
2A	Students read the information about the different forms of erosion and complete the sentences with a suitable verb phrase. **Key:** Shoes: this is because someone *wears them a lot*; pencil: this is because someone *uses it / writes with it a lot*.
2B	Students make a list of all the examples of wear erosion that can be seen in the classroom.
OVER TO YOU	**A** Students work in pairs to plan a trip to the Grand Canyon. They have a time limit and a budget of $150 dollars to spend when they arrive. Students should discuss their plans using the language prompts, and then make notes about the trip so that they can compare it to another group's and so that they have the material to be able to write a postcard to you. **B** Students write a postcard telling you about their trip.
Optional Extension	If you live near an area of natural beauty, you could do a short project on the formation of the area.
Homework Option	Students write about a school trip or family holiday to a national park or other such location.
Web links	www.nps.gov/grca Grand Canyon home page with information about geography, geology and things to do. www.nps.gov/yel/index.htm Yellowstone National Park information. www.nationalgeographic.com/earthpulse This site allows students to listen to the sounds made around the Great Barrier Reef.

THE CHILL ZONE 3

pp. 46-47

CRACK THE CODE!
Key: *Hello from Punxsutawney Phil.*

Song: "Camp Granada"

CD1 Track 25 **Audio script and key:**

Hello Mother, hello Father
Here I am at Camp Granada
Camp is very *entertaining*
And they say we'll have some fun if it stops *raining*

Now I don't want this should scare ya
But my bunk mate has malaria
You *remember* Jeffrey Hardy
They're about to organize a searching party

Take me *home*, oh Mother, Father
Take me *home*, I hate Granada
Don't leave me in the forest where
I might get eaten by a *bear*.

Wait a minute, it's stopped hailing.
Guys are *swimming*, guys are sailing
Playing *baseball*, gee that's better
Mother, Father kindly disregard this letter.

Swot spot:
Key: A. *wardrobe*, B. *bedside table*, C. *bed*, D. *bookcase*, E. *light*, F. *rug*.

Experiment!
Key: *the reaction creates a mini geyser / lava lamp.*

Shadows
Key: *an ice-cream; boots; trousers / jeans; a scarf; tea / coffee / cappuccino / any other hot drink; a tie.*

WORKING WITH TEXTS 3

pp. 48-49

National Parks in Danger

This is the third long text in a section aimed at preparing students for state examinations. The texts are graded according to level and are progressive. Each text is followed by a series of comprehension questions and work on summary skills. **Note:** the blanks are for the titles in exercise 3A.

Pronunciation note: Yosemite /yəˈsemɪtiː/

Before you read

1 Students should research the vocabulary before they read the text. This could be a dictionary activity as the rubric suggests, or you could look at the vocabulary together with the students.

Reading

2 Students read the texts and answer the comprehension questions.
Key:
1. *58.*
2. *Its sequoia (redwood) trees.*
3. *The Horseshoe Falls and the American / Bridal Falls.*
4. *The increase in the average global temperature.*
5. *Sea levels will rise.*
6. *Tropical forests will die.*
7. *Grizzly bears.*
8. *Seeds.*
9. *Glaciers are melting.*
10. *(Students choose two of the following.) Save electricity, take the bus to school or buy recycled products.*

Summary skills

3A Students match the titles to the paragraphs. This will help them to focus on the main point of each paragraph and so develop an important summary skill.
Key: *All about National Parks; The Biggest Dangers to National Parks; Effects of Global Warming on National Parks; Stopping Global Warming.*

3B Again, use of synonyms should be encouraged if students are to be successful in writing a summary.
Key: *wildlife / wild animals; enormous / very big; at risk / in danger; regions / areas; mist / fog; turning off / switching off.*

29

SCHOOL LIFE AND EDUCATION   LESSON **4A**

2B or not 2B? Classes, years and forms   pp. 50-51

This lesson looks at the school system in the USA, Ireland and the Caribbean.

Objectives: students will...	• learn / revise the lexis of the education system • learn about different examination and testing systems • compare their tests with those from other countries • write a letter to a penfriend explaining their country's school system
Warm-up	Students discuss what class they're in.
1	Students read the texts about school in the USA and Ireland. They complete the statements with key information from the texts. **Culture note:** there are regional differences in parts of the USA, as some states differ in the ages of compulsory education. This information represents the average system in the USA. **Key:** USA. The first year of Junior High School is the *sixth* grade. Students get their high school diploma when they're *18* years old. Ireland. Irish students start school aged *4*. They take short courses in their *transition* year.
2A CD1 Track 26	Give students a few moments to read through the text. Students listen for information about the ages Colette talks about. Students should listen to the track twice, as happens in international examinations. Check students' answers. **Audio script and key** (Accent: Carib) Hi I'm Colette, I'm *fifteen* years old and I'm at Secondary School in Barbados. Here Primary School starts when we're *four* and finishes at *eleven*. We have exams at *eleven*. Then we go to Secondary School. We have exams when we're *sixteen* – I have mine next year. After that we can leave school or choose to stay on until we're *eighteen*. When we're eighteen, we do more exams.
2B	**Key:** there are *12 years* of compulsory education in Barbados.
YOUR TURN	Students compare how many years are compulsory in their country.
3	Students look at the example test questions from other countries and attempt them. **Culture note:** this type of multiple choice test is centrally administered and is generally standardized by examination boards. The teachers do not grade their own students. **Key:** GSAT Jamaica - Social Studies: *B*; GSAT Jamaica - Science: *A*; 11+ Maths - Barbados: *£22.50*; AT New Zealand: *B*; Private school UK - Maths: *3,750*; 11+ non verbal - UK: *the first square*.
YOUR TURN	Students compare these exams with their own and look at difficulty.
OVER TO YOU	Students write a letter to Colette in Barbados explaining the education system in their country.
Optional Extension	Students research the school system in other countries in the ESW. The UK has not been dealt with here, neither have Australia or New Zealand. If you have links with a school in these countries, students could compile a list of questions to ask students in the school.
Homework Option	Students write a test similar to the GSAT test on a subject they are studying at the moment.
Web links	www.intense.co.uk Education and guardianship website to help find boarding schools in the UK. www.usastudyguide.com A student guide to education in the USA. www.immi.gov.au The Australian government guide to immigration and citizenship.

PEOPLE AND LIFESTYLES

LESSON 4B

Saturday Jobs — Kids who work

pp. 52-53

This lesson addresses the issue of children who work for pocket money or because of necessity.

Objectives: students will...	• learn / revise the lexis of jobs children do • learn about the law regarding child labour in the UK • compare the situation in the developing world • discuss what they can do to help stop child labour
Warm-up	Students discuss pocket money and the type of things they have to do to earn it. This is an opportunity to see how many students in the class have a part-time job.
1	Students look at the table to check the average pocket money in England. They then complete the table with their own situation. Students then discuss differences between theirs and the UK situation. **Note:** the information on the UK relates to 12-year-olds.
2	Students match the jobs to the pictures. **Key:** 1. *G*, 2. *E*, 3. *B*, 4. *C*, 5. *A*, 6. *H*, 7. *F*, 8. *D*.
YOUR TURN	Discussion of which jobs are boring and which are fun.
3A 3B **CD1 Track 27**	Give students a few moments to read through the questions. Students listen to Pete talking about the part-time job he does. Students should listen to the track twice, as happens in international examinations. When they first listen, students complete the general comprehension questions. **3A Key:** 1. *Pete is 13*; 2. *He works as a waiter*; 3. *He's saving up to buy a new computer*. When they listen for the second time, they listen for the number of hours he can legally work **3B Key:** 4. *Two hours*; 5. *Five hours*; 6. *Two hours*; 7. *Twenty-five hours*. **Audio script** (**Accent:** S. Eng) Hi, My name's Pete Whitehead and I'm thirteen. I work part-time in a coffee shop. I can't cook, I'm too young. I'm actually a waiter. The law says I can work 2 hours a day on school days. But I can't work after seven o'clock at night. I usually work from 4.30 to 6.30 after school. On Saturdays I can work for five hours, but on Sundays I can only work for two hours – but that's OK – I often have a lot of homework. In the school holidays I can work for twenty-five hours a week, if I want. I like earning money – I'm saving for a new computer.
4	Students read the information about child labour. Students answer the True / False / Doesn't say questions. **Key:** 1. *False*, 2. *True*, 3. *True*, 4. *Doesn't say*, 5. *False*, 6. *True*.
OVER TO YOU	Students work in pairs to organize a special event against child labour.
Optional Extension	Do a class survey after exercise 1, to compare results in the whole class. Students could write this up as a short report or express it as a bar or pie chart.
Homework Option	Students research child labour laws in their own country.
Web links	www.freethechildren.com Craig Kielburger's organization. www.thesource.me.uk/education_n_work For information about working laws and young people in the UK.

31

SPORT & LEISURE　　　　　　　　　　　　　　　　　　　　　　　　**LESSON 4C**

Read All About It! Magazines and newspapers pp. 54-55

This lesson introduces the topic of magazines and newspapers students read.

Objectives: students will...	• learn / revise the lexis of magazines and newspaper contents • learn / revise prepositions of place and some of time • learn about reading habits in the ESW • look at how newspapers are organized • write their own class magazine
Warm-up	Students discuss their favourite magazines and whether they (or their families) have a subscription to any.
1	Students do a reading activity to match the magazines to the description of their content. **Key:** 1. *F*, 2. *B*, 3. *D*, 4. *H*, 5. *G*, 6. *C*, 7. *E*, 8. *A*. **Culture note:** NME = New Musical Express
2A	Students complete the questionnaire related to their reading habits. They should just tick the first column at this stage. **Culture Note:** Q & A stands for Question and Answer and is a common feature of magazines and newspapers in the ESW.
2B CD1 Track 28	Students listen to Bryony and Stuart answering the questionnaire and tick the answers they give. Students should listen to the track twice, as happens in international examinations. **Audio script and key** (**Accents:** Int. = GB, Bryony = Eng, Stuart = USA.) INT.　　　Hi Briony, hi Stuart. Which types of magazines do you read? BRYONY　I like *travel magazines* like National Geographic, 'cos I like travelling and *fashion magazines* like Cosmo Girl 'cos they're fun. STUART　Yeah, I like *National Geographic* too, but I also read American Scientist. I love *science magazines*. INT.　　　Great, and where do you usually read, Stuart? STUART　Oh. *At home*. Sometimes I read a magazine when I'm waiting for the *dentist*. INT.　　　And you Briony? BRYONY　I often read magazines with *my friends, at my house or at their houses*, or at *school*. Sometimes I read on the *train* to school. STUART　I can't read on trains or buses! INT.　　　And when do you usually read your magazines? BRYONY　I buy Cosmo Girl every week, but I usually read it *at the weekends*. STUART　Oh, *at the weekends* for me too. INT.　　　What are your favourite pages in the magazines you read? BRYONY　I like the *features* and *interviews*. I like the *questionnaires* in Cosmo Girl too. STUART　Oh, the *interviews*. And I like the *features* too. And *question and answer pages*. I don't like crosswords though.
OVER TO YOU	Students work together to organize their own class magazine. **Tip:** this could be regarded as a project to be completed over a period of time so much of the work could be done at home, except for the organization and distribution of tasks.
Optional Nip and Tuck	If time is short, you could have the groups designing only the front page of a newspaper or magazine or a website related to the magazine.
Homework Option	Students work on writing one feature from a newspaper or magazine.
Web links	www.nationalgeographic.com The geography magazine's website. www.skateboardermag.com A website from a skateboarding magazine. www.world-newspapers.com/youth.html A listings page of teen magazines around the world.

HISTORY AND TRADITIONS

LESSON 4D

The Origins of English
The history of the language pp. 56-57

This lesson provides a simplified introduction to the history of the English language.

Objectives: students will...	• learn about borrowed words in English • learn about the history of place names • learn about the origins of the English language • compare English words used in students' own language
Warm-up CD1 Track 29	Students look at and listen to the pronunciation of the name of this village on Anglesey Island, in North Wales. For the **audio script**, see photo on Student's Book page 56. The aim is to show how different Welsh and English are and to introduce the concept of Celtic languages. **Pronunciation note:** 'Celtic' changes meaning according to pronunciation. | Celtic (Scottish football team) | /ˈseltɪk/ | | Celtic (tribe) | /ˈkeltɪk/ |
1A	Students read and extract the information from the text to draw arrows to show where the Jutes, Angles and Saxons arrived. **Key:** Angles – *East coast*; Jutes – *South coast*; Saxons – *South East*.
1B	Students answer True / False questions. This will provide an opportunity to practise the pronunciation of the points of the compass. **Key:** 1. *False*, 2. *True*, 3. *False*, 4. *False*.
2A	Students use the sample Runic alphabet to write their own names. This shows the difference between the modern alphabet and the oldest one.
2B	Allow students to have fun writing a message using the Runic alphabet which other students can then decipher.
3	Students look at the place-name endings and find examples of these places on the map. **Note:** the places actually demonstrate where invaders from different cultures arrived in the UK e.g. there are a lot of Norse villages in the East. **Key:** castra: *Chester, Leicester, Gloucester, Colchester, Manchester, Worcester* forda: *Stafford, Oxford, Watford, Chelmsford, Guildford* by: *Whitby, Grimsby, Derby*
4A 4B CD1 Track 30	Students guess the language these English borrowed words come from and their meaning. Then they listen to check. **Audio script and key** (Accent: GB) A pizza is *a flat bread often with tomato and cheese.* It's an *Italian* word. A bungalow is *a house with only a ground floor.* It's a *Hindi* word. An anorak is *a coat.* The word is *Inuit*. A hooligan is *a violent person.* It's a *Celtic* word. A frankfurter is *a type of sausage.* It's *German*. A tsunami is *a very big wave.* The word is *Japanese*. A kangaroo is *an Australian animal.* It's an *Aboriginal* word. A rendezvous is *a meeting place.* The word is *French*.
OVER TO YOU	Students work in pairs to make a list of English words used in their language. **Tip:** if you have a multi-ethnic class, you could compare this with other languages.
Optional Extension	Other place names to pinpoint and research on maps of the UK include -thorpe, -nook. Students compare how many they have found.
Homework Option	Students collect more examples of English words from newspapers and television programmes and advertisements.
Web links	www.alttext.com This is a blog with links to information about Tolkien and runes. www.llanfairpwllgwyngyllgogerychwyrndrobwllllantysiliogogogoch.co.uk A website dedicated to the village with the longest name in the UK.

33

THE WORLD WE LIVE IN

LESSON 4E

Unsolved Mysteries
Places with legends and mysteries — pp. 58-59

This lesson introduces some of the places in the ESW with a reputation for mystery.

Objectives: students will...	• learn about Loch Ness and the Bermuda Triangle • give opinions on the various mysteries • draw personal conclusions on the basis of evidence presented • carry out a KET-style speaking task
Warm-up	Students discuss whether they believe in ghosts or monsters.
1	Students read the text about Loch Ness and the monster and answer the questions. **Key:** 1. *B*, 2. *C*, 3. *A*, 4. *C*.
YOUR TURN	Students look at the pictures and use the prompts to discuss probable explanations for the Loch Ness monster sightings. They should be encouraged to speculate.
2A CD1 Track 31	Give students a few moments to read through the short text and look at the photos. Students listen to two stories about disappearances in the Bermuda Triangle. Students should listen to the track twice, as happens in international examinations. Check students' answers. **Audio script and key** (Accents: GB) Story 1 On December the 5th 1945, 5 American aeroplanes left Florida together. The name of this group of planes was *Flight 19*. They contacted Florida several times. Then they just disappeared… they were in the Bermuda Triangle. Story 2 In March 1918 an American Navy boat left Brazil to go back to the United States. The ship never arrived in America. It disappeared in the Bermuda Triangle. Its name was the *USS Cyclops*.
2B	Students read the opinions and possible explanations of the disappearances in the Bermuda Triangle. Students then discuss their own views using the prompts or their own ideas to speculate.
OVER TO YOU	Students work in pairs to do this KET-style speaking activity. Student A looks at the poster about England's most haunted house. Student B asks questions using the prompts on the page and Student A answers. Students then swap roles.
Optional Extension	Students research further mysterious disappearances in the Bermuda Triangle.
Homework Option	Student write a ghost story or invent a Loch Ness Monster sighting.
Web links	www.lochness.co.uk This has a 24 hour webcam with views over Loch Ness. www.owls.org Information about the World Owl Trust. www.muncaster.co.uk Information about Muncaster Castle.

THE CHILL ZONE 4

pp. 60-61

Are you a polyglot?
Key: 1. *Spanish*, 2. *Russian*, 3. *Chinese*, 4. *French*, 5. *German*, 6. *Portuguese*, 7. *English*, 8. *Latin*.

Swot spot:
Key: 1. *b*, 2. *c*, 3. *b*.

Are you a mathematical genius?
Key: *29* (add 7 each time); *6* (halve the number each time); *18* (add 2 then 3 then 4 then 5); *18* (the second number and the solution make the next sum, 3+4=7, 4+7=11, 7+11=18).

WORKING WITH TEXTS 4

pp. 62-63

Stonehenge – Who built it? What's it for?

This is the fourth long text in a section aimed at preparing students for state examinations. The texts are graded according to level and are progressive. Each text is followed by a series of comprehension questions and work on summary skills.

Before you read

1 Students check the meanings of some of the difficult words in the text using their dictionary. They should also look at the different meanings given for the word 'earth'.

Reading

2 Students read the text and answer the questions.
Key:
1. *Salisbury*; 2. *A circular area made of earth*; 3. *2150 BC*; 4. *People pulled them with rollers and ropes*; 5. *30 stones weighing 50 tonnes each*; 6. *Probably about 20 million*; 7. *Merlin*; 8. *Midsummer's Day / The Summer Solstice*; 9. *An alien airport or landing place*; 10. *A replica of Stonehenge made in America from cars*.

Summary skills

3A Students fill the gaps to complete the text.
Key:
Stonehenge is a famous prehistoric stone circle in *England / Salisbury*. People started building Stonehenge in *3100* BC. There are many stones; there are *82* stones from the Preseli Mountains and *30* Sarsen Stones. The building of Stonehenge probably took about *20* million hours. There are different interpretations of the use of Stonehenge. In the past, people thought it was build by a *giant* for Merlin. Today, some people think it is an astronomical *observatory* or a temple. A few people think it is an alien *airport*. There are many replicas of Stonehenge all over the world.

3B One of the many practical summary skills that students need is that of being able to summarize a text sufficiently to be able to perform a search on Internet engines such as Google.
Key:
The last sentence is the most precise. There is no need to use capital letters when using a search engine and inverted commas narrow your search.

35

SCHOOL LIFE AND EDUCATION

LESSON 5A

What's Cool in School?
School fashion and school rules — pp. 64-65

This lesson introduces two aspects of school culture in the UK, school uniforms and school rules and punishments.

Objectives: students will...	• learn / revise the lexis of rules and regulations • give opinions about school uniforms • learn about school uniforms and school rules	• compare punishments in the UK with their own • discuss lockers and locker culture
Warm-up	Ask students whether uniforms exist in their countries. If not, ask whether there is a specific dress code. **Culture note:** uniforms are still the norm in the UK, although they are often less formal than they were in the past.	
1A	Students read and match the quotes to the photos. **Culture note:** hoodies are tops with a hood. They are associated in some places with violence and aggressive behaviour. People wearing hoodies are banned from some shopping centres in the UK. **Key:** 1. *A*, 2. *E*, 3. *D*, 4. *C*, 5. *B*, 6. *F*.	
1B CD1 Track 32	Give students a few moments to read through the good and bad points about school uniforms. Students listen for Vikki's opinion. Students should listen to the track twice, as happens in international examinations. Check students' answers. Students add more good and bad points about school uniform to the lists. **Key:** Bad points: *ties are uncomfortable, girls look stupid in ties, uniforms are really old-fashioned*. Good points: *you don't have to decide what to wear in the morning*. **Audio script (Accent: Eng)** I hate wearing a uniform! I think ties are really uncomfortable, especially in summer and girls look really stupid in ties. I also think our uniform is really old-fashioned. The skirts are really long and I don't like the shirts very much. My Mum's school uniform was practically the same! Are there any good points? Well, every morning's the same so you don't have to choose your clothes in the morning, but that's about all.	
2	Students look at the list of school rules and tick the ones related to school uniform. **Key:** No trainers, no short skirts, no collars up, no big ties, no top button undone, no blazers inside out.	
YOUR TURN	Students look at the rules again and compare them with their own schools. They then evaluate whether the rules are sensible or stupid.	
3A	This exercise looks at typical punishments from the UK for breaking school rules. Check that the students understand the punishments. **Culture note:** it's common for teachers in the USA to give lines as a punishment as well. Students may have seen this punishment in TV programmes like "The Simpsons".	
3B CD1 Track 33	Students choose a punishment from the list to match the "crime". They then listen to the students talking and see if they matched the crimes and punishments correctly. **Audio script and key (Accents:** 1. USA, 2. Aus, 3. USA, 4. Ind, 5. Irish, 6. Scot, 7. Eng.) 1. "I yawned three times in a class and the teacher made me *stand outside* for the rest of the lesson" 2. "I didn't do my homework so the teacher gave me *double homework* the next day" 3. "I texted my friend in class so my teacher put me in the *isolation booth* all day" 4. "We passed some notes around in class so we got a *one hour detention* – the whole class!" 5. "I didn't eat my school lunch so I got a horrible *telling-off*" 6. "I cheated in my exam. It was awful they gave me three days' *exclusion* from school" 7. "My mobile phone rang in class. They *telephoned my Mum*. She was furious!"	
YOUR TURN	Students have the opportunity to evaluate whether the punishments were fair or unfair.	
OVER TO YOU	Students have the chance to imagine what they would do if they had a locker at school. Point out that the **Did you Know?** box has more information about lockers.	
Optional Extensions	• Students could design their own school uniform and write a description of it. • Students could discuss punishments for "crimes" they commit at home.	
Homework Option	Students write about why their teachers or parents get angry.	
Web links	www.news.bbc.co.uk/cbbcnews Uniforms and school rules around the world. www.schooluniforms.co.uk A shop which retails school uniforms. www.sloughgrammar.berks.sch.uk All about an English school.	

PEOPLE AND LIFESTYLES **LESSON 5B**

Tea Time — Family Mealtimes pp. 66-67

This lesson introduces discussion about food habits in the ESW.

Objectives: students will...	• learn / revise the lexis of mealtimes • learn / revise the lexis of breakfast foods • learn about cultural differences related to mealtimes • compare their own food culture with that of others • do a food quiz
Warm-up	Students discuss their main meal and where they eat it.
1A	Students read the extracts from guides to the ESW and match the countries to the texts **Key:** *Australia, The UK, The USA.*
1B	The focus is on comprehension as they answer the questions. **Key:** 1. *Australia*, 2. *The UK*, 3. *The UK*, 4. *The USA.*
1C CD1 Track 34	Give students a few moments to read through the text. Students listen for the missing information about Ireland. Students should listen to the track twice, as happens in international examinations. Check students' answers. **Note:** Students may need to listen several times; the activity is demanding. **Audio script and Key** (**Accent:** Italian) I went to *Ireland*. Back at home in Italy, we usually have dinner at 8 o'clock, but when you eat with a family in Ireland, you usually eat early in the evening. My Irish family had dinner at around *6 o'clock*. The parents in the family had *tea or coffee* with their dinner. The kids had *milk or juice*. Manners are important in Ireland, you don't start eating until *everyone is ready to start*. You must remember to say 'please' and 'thank you'. The family was really nice, but there was never any *bread* on the table! That was really difficult for me because I usually have *bread* with my dinner.
YOUR TURN	Students fill in the tourist guide information for their country.
2A 2B CD1 Track 35	Students complete this food quiz about food in the ESW. They then listen and check. **Language note:** to 'know your onions' = to be an expert in something **Audio script and Key** (**Accent:** GB) 1. In Britain you usually drink *tea with milk* 2. In Canada and the USA, one of the most popular things to have for breakfast is *pancakes with maple syrup* 3. In the USA people eat TV dinners *in the living room* 4. A poppadom is a delicious *Indian crisp bread* 5. In the UK, *tomato and egg* is NOT a flavour of crisps
OVER TO YOU	**A** Students look at the international breakfasts in the table and decide which they would prefer to eat. **B** They then discuss the type of breakfast they usually have.
Optional Extension	Work with the students on writing a recipe related to a typical dish from your country.
Homework Options	• Students research typical food in a country not mentioned in the lesson such as New Zealand or the Caribbean. • They could research a typical American breakfast as menus tend to be very extensive.
Web links	www.thedunesrestaurant.com A restaurant serving American breakfasts. www.lifeintheusa.com A guide to everyday life in America.

SPORT & LEISURE

LESSON 5C

Goal! Sport in the English-speaking world
pp. 68-69

This lesson explores typical sports in the ESW. Some of the sports will be well-known to the students and others will be unfamiliar.

Objectives: students will...	• learn / revise the lexis of sports • learn / revise the lexis of sports equipment • learn about popular sports in the ESW • write about how to play a sport
Warm-up	Students look at the pictures and try to identify the sports. **Key:** (from left to right) *baseball, Australian rules football, American football, cricket.*
1A	Students label the pictures. **Key:** *gloves, helmet, bats, boots with studs, pads.*
1B	Students read the texts and label the pictures. **Key:** from left to right: Where: *American football, cricket, baseball, Australian rules football* Ball: *baseball, American football, Australian rules football, cricket* Equipment: *cricket, Australian rules football, American football, baseball*
2 CD1 Track 36	Give students a few moments to read through the information in the table. Students listen for the missing information. Students should listen to the track twice, as happens in international examinations. Check students' answers. **Audio script and key** (**Accents:** 1. Aus, 2. Ind, 3. USA, 4. USA.) People play Australian Rules Football in Australia, obviously, but also in *Canada* and *New Zealand*. Oh and there's a league in *Ireland* too. Games have four quarters. Each quarter lasts *20 minutes*. There are *eighteen* players on each side. People shout "goaaaaal!" when there's a goal. People play cricket all over the world including England, *Australia*, *India*, Pakistan, *South Africa* and the West Indies. Games are very long. They last from *one day to five days*! There are *eleven* players on a cricket team. The cricket shout is "Howzat?" when a batsman is out. People play baseball all over the world. It's the American national sport. Games last on average *3 hours*. There are *nine* players on a baseball team. People shout "strike out!". American football is really popular in the US and in *Canada*. Games are long because of the tactics. But, there are four quarters in a game and each lasts *fifteen minutes*. Oh yes, there are *53 players* in an American Football team, but only eleven people can play at the same time. People shout "touch down!".
OVER TO YOU	Students write about a team sport they know. They should use the information in the table in exercise 2 to guide them. They can then compare their answers with another group.
Did you know? CD1 Track 37	For the Princeton Chant **audio script**, see Student's Book page 69.
Optional Extension	Students write about their favourite sports team and players.
Homework Option	Students research some American baseball teams from the Internet. They could find out about the team, its home ground and its fans.
Web links	www.afl.com.au Australian rules football league. www.nfl.com American football league. www.cricinfo.com Cricket information.

38

HISTORY AND TRADITIONS **LESSON 5D**

Pancake Day — Spring and summer festivals

pp. 70-71

This lesson introduces some of the most widely celebrated spring and summer festivals from the ESW.

Objectives: students will...	• learn / revise the lexis of celebrations • learn about Pancake Day, July 4th, Easter, May Day, St. Patrick's Day, April Fool's Day and The Notting Hill Carnival • compare ESW festivals with their own • discuss what to do for World Students' Day
Warm-up	Students discuss their favourite festivals.
1A	Students read the texts and match them with their appropriate headlines. **Key:** *The Notting Hill Carnival, Shrove Tuesday or Pancake Day, Easter, St. Patrick's Day, May Day.*
1B	This is a certification-style True / False / Doesn't say reading text. **Key:** 1. *False*, 2. *Doesn't say*, 3. *True*, 4. *True*, 5. *False*.
2 CD1 Track 38	Give students a few moments to read through the information in the table. Students listen for information about what Sandy and Rick do on July 4th. Students should listen to the track twice, as happens in international examinations. Check students' answers. **Language note:** "eat barbecue" is an American expression. In British English the expression is "have a barbecue". **Audio script and key** (Accents: USA) SANDY I love the 4th of July. It's my favourite holiday. The weather's usually good so we *eat barbecue* with the family. In the afternoon I *go to the baseball* game with my Dad and sometimes my brother comes too. In the stadium there's always a fireworks display at the end of the game, so yeah, we *watch the fireworks*. RICK Oh yeah, the 4th of July is Independence Day so we have a good day. It's a holiday so we *eat a lot*. We usually *go out for a picnic* with all the family – if the weather's good. Then we often *play baseball* together. Sometimes we *watch the baseball game on TV*. Then my Dad usually has *some fireworks* so we watch them together.
YOUR TURN	Students decide whether they would prefer a picnic or a barbecue.
3A	Elicit from the students whether they do anything special to celebrate April 1st. Check that they understand the meaning of 'practical jokes'.
3B	Students match the short texts about April Fool's Day activities to the pictures. **Note:** these are all true events. **Key:** 1. *B*, 2. *C*, 3. *A*, 4. *D*.
OVER TO YOU	Students work together to plan a celebration for World Students' Day. They could then compare their work with that of another group.
Optional Extension	Ask students about any practical jokes they have played or they know about.
Homework Option	Students write about the most recent festival they have celebrated.
Web links	www.derbyshireuk.net Tourist information site for Derbyshire. www.londoncarnival.co.uk The official Notting Hill Carnival website. www.july4th.org All about Boston's American Independence Day celebrations.

THE WORLD WE LIVE IN
LESSON 5E

Evolution — Darwin and the environment
pp. 72-73

This lesson explores the topic of evolution and looks at a biography of Charles Darwin. **Tip:** this topic is particularly suited to cross-curricular work with a science teacher.

Objectives: students will...	• learn / revise the lexis of evolution • learn about evolution • learn about endangered species • consider man's impact on the environment • extrapolate from a text to draw a route on a map
Warm-up CD1 Track 39	Students study the definition of evolution and then match the labels to the pictures of the horse's evolution. They then listen and check. **Audio script and key** (Accent: Eng) The first picture is of the *Hyracotherium*. It lived 50 million years ago. Picture two is of the *Mesohippus* from 30 million years ago. Then there is the *Merychippus*. It lived 20 million years ago. The last picture is of *Equus* – today's horse.
1A	**Note:** you will need to **make photocopies of the map** on page 77 of this Teacher's Book. Students read and listen to the text and draw the route on the map. **Key:** the finished map should look like this: **Tip:** bring in maps of the world to help students, or check that they are available in the classroom.
1B	Students answer the True / False / Doesn't say questions. **Key:** 1. *False*, 2. *True*, 3. *False*, 4. *Doesn't say*, 5. *Doesn't say*.
2A	The students work out the answers to the questions. **Key:** Which moth is easier to see? *The second*. Why? *It's looks white against the tree trunk*. Which moth will probably become extinct? *The second. Predators will see it*.
2B 2C CD1 Track 40	The story of the peppered moth is often quoted as a striking example of evolution. Students try to figure out why one particular moth would be more common at each of these times in history. They then listen to check their answers. **Audio script and key** (Accent: GB) Picture 1. Before the industrial revolution, buildings and trees were clean. *The white peppered moth was more common*. Picture 2. During the industrial revolution, the air was black. The buildings were black. The trees were black. *The black peppered moth was more common*. Picture 3. After the Clean Air Act, buildings and trees were clean again. Guess which moth was more common! Yes, that's right… *the white peppered moth*. This is how man affects evolution.
3	Students read the text and match the pictures to the texts. **Key:** • Name the animals: A. *tiger*, B. *fox*, C. *panda*, D. *dodo*. • Match facts to animals: 1. *B*, 2. *D*, 3. *C*, 4. *A*.
OVER TO YOU	Students work together to make a list of endangered species and protected animals in the world and in their country.
Optional Extension	Students do further research on one of the endangered species in exercise 3. They could look at why the species is endangered and what people can do to protect it.
Homework Option	Students use an encyclopaedia or the Internet to find out more about the Galapagos Islands.
Web links	www.aboutdarwin.com Information on the life and studies of Darwin. www.bbc.co.uk/sn BBC science and nature site. www.nhm.ac.uk The Natural History Museum in London.

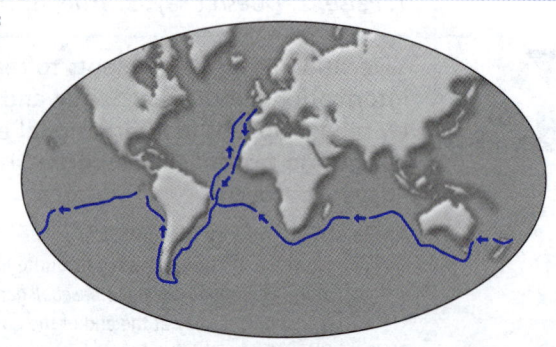

THE CHILL ZONE 5

pp. 74-75

CD1 Track 41 For the rhyme **audio script** see Student's Book page 74.

Txting!
Key: the answers are upside down at the bottom of the exercise.

HIDE AND SEEK!!
Key: the animal is an owl.

Recipe
Key: 1. C, 2. A, 3. E, 4. G, 5. F or D, 6. B, 7. D or F.
The correct answer for 5 is F and for 7 is D but students may have trouble with the graphic.

Darwin Swot spot
Key: 1. c, 2. c, 3. a, 4. b, 5. a.

CLOTHESWORD!
Key: Across: 2. *jersey*; 3. *pads*; 5. *gloves*; 6. *boots*; 7. *helmet*; 8. *shirts*.
Down: 1. *cap*; 2. *jumper*; 4. *shorts*; 6. *bat*.

WORKING WITH TEXTS 5

pp. 76-77

Proms and Homecoming

This is the fifth long text in a section aimed at preparing students for state examinations. The texts are graded according to level and are progressive. Each text is followed by a series of comprehension questions and work on summary skills.

Before you read

1 Students use the picture to identify difficult words from the text.
Key: A. bonfire, B. bow tie, C. ball gown, D. dinner jacket.

Reading

2 Students read the texts and answer the FAQs.
Pronunciation note: students should know that the individual letters in FAQs are sounded:
F.A.Qs /ef/ /eɪ/ /kjuːz/

Key:
1. A formal dance to celebrate leaving school.
2. Formal clothes. (Boys wear dinner jackets and bow ties. Girls wear ball gowns.)
3. There's a dinner and a dance.
4. Australia, New Zealand and Ireland.
5. A celebration for people who have left school or college.
6. Election of the king and queen, a bonfire party and parade, a ball, a sports game.
7. No. Some people think they are expensive and old-fashioned.

Summary skills

3A Students match the synonyms.
Key: *dance / ball; formal / smart; hire / rent; festival / celebration; game / match; band / orchestra.*

3B Students base their summary on the answers to the comprehension questions. They should be reminded to use connectors to make their summaries more cohesive.

SCHOOL LIFE AND EDUCATION   LESSON **6A**

What did you get? I got a B — School reports and grades
pp. 78-79

This lesson introduces grading, state exams, school reports and marks.

Objectives: students will...	• learn / revise the lexis of school subjects • correct a student's history test • compare reports and grading • work out a mathematical average
Warm-up	Students discuss their testing system. They also discuss the type of exams they prefer, written or oral. You could make a list of state exams on the board.
1	This is intended as a speed activity to help improve dictionary and general reference skills. Students match the acronyms to the full name of the exam. **Key:** Owl = Ordinary Wizarding Level (The Wizard World – from Harry Potter), SAT = Scholastic Assessment Test (USA, Canada), GSAT = Grade Six Achievement Test (Jamaica), ICSE = Indian Certificate of Secondary Education (India), NCEA = National Certificate of Educational Achievement (New Zealand).
2A CD2 Track 2	Students read the school report from Australia and match the subjects with the section of the report. They then listen to check the subjects and grades. **Note:** the listening is relatively fast to stretch more talented students, so weaker groups may need to hear it more than twice. **Audio script and key** (Accents: Aus) STUDENT A — What grades did you get on your report? STEPHEN — Let's see in *English* I got a grade B, *Maths* grade C, *Science* also grade C, *Art and design*, oh dear, a D. STUDENT A — Oops. STEPHEN — *I.C.T.* hooray! I got an A. STUDENT A — Great! STEPHEN — *Citizenship* grade C, *P.E.* oops Grade E.
2B	Students complete the comprehension questions on the text. **Key:** 1. *True*, 2. *True*, 3. *False*, 4. *Doesn't say*.
2C	Students look at the percentages on the school report and work out Stephen's average. **Key:** 59.4%
3	Students look at the way teachers express grades in the ESW.
YOUR TURN	Students compare these methods with their own.
OVER TO YOU	**A** Students see a part of Stephen's history text. They read the text and use the timeline to help them correct his work. **Key:** ~~William of Normandy~~: Harold Hardrada; ~~Harold Hardrada~~: Harold Godwin; ~~September 1079~~: October 1066; William of Normandy: right; ~~Edward the Confessor~~: William of Normandy. **B** Students assess the work and give him a percentage and a grade or a mark out of ten.
Optional Extension	Students write reports for each other as if they were the teacher.
Homework Option	Students write a short paragraph entitled "Exams and Tests".
Web links	www.jis.gov.jm/gov_ja/education.asp An education site from the Jamaican government. www.usastudyguide.com Information about American assessments tests and studying in the USA.

PEOPLE AND LIFESTYLES   LESSON **6B**

Home Sweet Home   Types of homes   pp. 80-81

This lesson addresses the types of homes which can be found in the ESW.

Objectives: students will...	• learn / revise the lexis of houses • learn / revise the lexis of rooms within the house • learn about unusual places to live • compare advantages and disadvantages of different types of dwelling • discuss their own homes
Warm-up	Students talk about the type of place where they live.
1A	Ask students to tick the boxes of the things they have at home and monitor their answers.
1B CD2 Track 3	Give students a few moments to look at the pictures. Students should listen to the track twice, as happens in international examinations. The first time they listen, they should match the person to the house. **Key:** cattle station *1*; narrow boat *2*; Jamaican home *3*; log cabin *4*.
1C CD2 Track 3	The second time students listen, they should say which things from the list in 1A the speakers have. **Note:** the speakers talk about things they don't have, as well as things they do have. **Audio script and key** (Accents: Kelly = Aus, Jimmy = Eng, Louisa = Carib, Trevor = USA.) Hi, my name's Kelly. We live on a cattle station in Australia. It's quite big, because there are fifteen of us who live there. I like the *games room* and the *living room*. There are two big *kitchens* as well. Outside we have the *helipad* but we don't have a swimming pool in the *garden*. Hello, my name's Jimmy. From April to November we live on a narrow boat. We travel along the canals in England. There's quite a lot of space on the boat, we have a *bathroom* and 2 *bedrooms*. There's a little *kitchen* and a small *living room*. I miss the garden 'cos I can't play football. My name's Louisa and I'm from Jamaica. Our house is quite traditional and I really like it. The thing I like best is the *garden* – there's lots of space and we often eat outside on the *terrace*. Hi, I'm Trevor. My aunt lives in a log cabin in the Rocky Mountains, here in the USA. We often visit her at weekends and in the holidays. I like the cabin because there are beautiful views from the *bedroom*s and there's a *hot tub* in the *garden*.
2A	Students say whether they would like to live in these places as a pre-reading activity.
2B	This is a reading activity where students match the text to the picture. **Key:** 1. *C*, 2. *B*, 3. *A*.
2C	Ask students to read the texts again and extract the information about advantages and disadvantages of living in each of these places according to the texts. | KEY	advantages	disadvantages
---	---	---
lighthouse	on the beach great for surfing	long way to the town centre cold in winter a lot of steps & no lift
windmill	friends like it fantastic view	difficult to put pictures on walls lots of steps and no lift
horse-drawn caravan	the garden changes every day	it's small it has no electricity	
3	Students calculate the areas. **Key:** bedroom: *16.77 m²*; living room: *17.63 m²*; bathroom: *4.59 m²*; kitchen: *8.64 m²*; bedroom: *6.66 m²*; balcony: *4.25 m²*. Total area: *58.54 m²*.
OVER TO YOU	Students work together to make lists of the things they like and don't like about their homes.
Optional Extension	Discuss the advantages and disadvantages of living in a trailer (static caravan of the type which is common in some states in the USA) or another unusual place (cave, space station, oil rig at sea).
Homework Option	Students write a description of their house to include the good and bad points looked at in the **Over to You** section.
Web links	www.canalmuseum.org.uk A site dedicated to narrow boats. www.future-systems.com A site about an award-winning house of the future. www.horsecaravans.co.uk A site for those wanting to book holidays in a horse-drawn caravan.

SPORT & LEISURE

LESSON 6C

It's just a Craze — Crazes through the ages

pp. 82-83

This lesson looks at crazes today and throughout history.

Objectives: students will...	• learn / revise the lexis of chess and other activities • learn / revise the lexis of protective clothing • learn about the history of the yoyo and other crazes • order events chronologically • make a survey of current crazes
Warm-up	Ask students whether they can use a yoyo and how proficient they are.
1	Students match the period in history to the drawings of the yoyo in use. Check their answers. **Key:** A. *4*, B. *3*, C. *6*, D. *1*, E. *2*, F. *5*.
2	This is a quiz on the subject of chess. This game has been undergoing a revival in the last two or three years in the ESW. **Key:** 1. *a*; 2. most sources state China *a*; 3. these are all characters from Harry Potter *b*; 4. *D* = pawn, *B* = castle, *E* = knight, *F* = bishop, *C* = queen, *A* = king.
YOUR TURN	An optional activity would be to set up a chess competition in the class to see who is the best player.
3	Students match the protective clothing to the picture. **Key** (in clockwise order from the top): *elbow pads, helmet, knee pads, trainers, wrist-guards*.
4A 4B CD2 Track 4	This activity widens the subject of crazes. Students guess when the craze was at its height. They then listen and check. **Key:** roller skating *A*, hula hoop *C*, skipping *B*, Rollerblading *G*, cycling *D*, marbles *F*, Rubik's cube *E*. **Audio script** (**Accent:** Eng) Well the oldest of these crazes is actually marbles. The ancient Egyptians played marbles about 2700 BC. The next oldest is skipping. The Chinese invented skipping in 770 BC. Then comes roller-skating. This was very popular in the 1840s, in the Victorian age. Cycling was the next craze. That started around 1865. Then we move into the twentieth century with the hula hoop which was very popular in the 1950s. The Rubik's cube was a phenomenon of the 1980s. The most recent of these crazes was rollerblading in the 1990s.
4C	Students now write the crazes in chronological order. This activity is designed to familiarize students with dates and ages and help them place these ages in terms of chronology. **Key:** 1. *marbles*, 2. *skipping*, 3. *roller skating*, 4. *cycling*, 5. *hula hoop*, 6. *Rubik's cube*, 7. *Rollerblading*.
OVER TO YOU	Students discuss their current crazes. In 2007 scoobies, chess, sudoku and its variations were the main crazes in the UK.
Optional Extension	Students choose another board game such as Scrabble, Risk, Cluedo or Monopoly and describe how to play.
Homework Option	Research the history of the bicycle.
Web links	www.nationalyoyo.org This is an American site dedicated to the yoyo. www.scoobies.net About the recent craze for scoubidou. www.pedalinghistory.com The history of the bicycle. www.jumpropeinstitute.com An American site about skipping.

HISTORY AND TRADITIONS

LESSON 6D

Starting a New Life
Immigration in the age of the steamship

pp. 84-85

This lesson explores the issue of immigration and the difficulties faced by past migrants to Australia, the UK and the USA. **Note:** it provides an excellent opportunity for students to empathise with any recent immigrants there may be in their class or school.

Objectives: students will...	• learn / revise the lexis of travelling • learn about immigration in the last century • write a letter home from abroad • discuss what to take on a journey abroad
Warm-up	Students discuss living in a different country and whether they would like this or not. **Tip:** encourage any students who are recent immigrants to contribute to the discussion.
1A 1B	**Culture note:** the picture of the steamship is of the SS Great Britain built by Isambard Kingdom Brunel. It can be visited in the port of Bristol. This is a pre-reading activity. Focus on the information about Australia in the box. Encourage students to try and guess the answers to the questions before they read the texts. Ask students to cover the texts if necessary. Have a feedback session. Students read the text to check their answers against the correct ones. **Key:** 1. How long did the journey take in 1860? *65 days average*; 2. What did steerage passengers take with them? *Clothes, food, bedclothes, some other possessions*; 3. What did steerage passengers do on the journey? *They played games (cards), played musical instruments, danced, children did lessons, people wrote letters and diaries;* 4. What did steerage passengers eat? *Meat, biscuits, rice and potatoes;* 5. What problems did they have? *Seasickness, fever, smell, noise of animals, heat and cold, uncomfortable journey;* 6. How much coal was there on the ship? *1,000 tonnes.*
YOUR TURN	Focus on the information about immigration to the USA. Students complete the landing card similar to one they would have had to complete at Ellis Island.
WEB PROJECT	Ellis Island. Information about Ellis Island can be found by following the link in the box. **Note: Working with Texts 6** is all about immigration to Ellis Island, which could be incorporated into the project.
2 CD2 Track 5	Give students a few moments to read through the problems listed on the page. You could elicit possible problems given that Paul left the West Indies to go to Britain in 1952. Students should listen to the track twice, as happens in international examinations. Check students' answers. **Key:** *the cold weather, the different food, city life, racism, missing his family.* **Audio script (Accent:** Carib) The first problem was that it was very cold in Britain. In Jamaica, it's hot. Everybody says the same. It really was very cold. Then the food was different. The food was OK but it was different from home in Jamaica. The other big problem was the life. I lived in a village in Jamaica. When I came to Britain I lived in London. Life in the city was very difficult at first. There were a few problems with racism. The majority of people were OK, but there were some problems at the beginning. Of course, I really missed my mother, my father and my brothers.
OVER TO YOU	Students imagine that they are travelling to a new life in Australia on a steamship. Remind them that the journey would probably take more than 65 days. Students plan what they would pack, what they would do on the journey and what they would miss about their home country. Again, this could provide a good opportunity to talk about experiences of recent immigrants to your country. Students write a letter home to their family from their imaginary trip. **Note:** this is a KET-style writing activity.
Optional Extension	Students do a project on immigration to their country or emigration from it.
Homework Option	Students write a diary entry for the day they arrive in Australia, the UK or the USA as an immigrant.
Web links	www.ssgreatbritain.org All about Brunel's famous ship. www.akvhs.org/their_journey_to_america.htm Information regarding immigrants' journeys to America, particularly Pennsylvania. http://immigration.museum.vic.gov.au/education The Australian government's official educational website relating to immigration. www.titanic.com Facts and figures about the Titanic disaster.

45

THE WORLD WE LIVE IN
LESSON 6E

One Small Step... Exploration: sea, land and space pp. 86-87

This lesson addresses famous explorers and explorations.

Objectives: students will...	• learn / revise the lexis of types of journeys • read an article about an historic event • learn about the moon landings and the race for the South Pole • extract information from a map • discuss what to take on a survival trip
Warm-up CD2 Track 6	Students read and listen to Neil Armstrong's first words from the Moon. **Key:** *C. on the the Moon.* **Audio script (Accent: USA)** "Houston. Tranquillity Base here. The eagle has landed…that's one small step for a man… one giant leap for mankind." **Note:** many people believe that the quotation is "one small step for man" (not "a man"). Official sources add the article 'a'!
1A 1B CD2 Track 7	Encourage students to guess when these events happened. They then listen to check their answers. **Key and extra information:** 1. The first men to climb Mount Everest – 29 May *1953* Edmund Hillary (NZ) and Tenzing Norgay (Sherpa - Nepal); 2. The first submarine trip – *1620* Dutchman Cornelius Drebell. River Thames; 3. The first non-stop transatlantic flight Alcock and Brown *1919*; 4. The first flight around the world – *1924* (175 days); 5. The first hot air balloon flight round the world was in *2002*; 6. The first people to travel around the world by land visiting both poles started their journey in 1979 and finished in *1982*. **Audio script (Accent: Eng)** Well. In chronological order. The first submarine trip in the River Thames was in 1620. That's very early, isn't it? Then we have the first transatlantic flight non-stop, that was in 1919. The next of these events is the first flight around the world. That was 1924. Then there were the first men to reach the top of Mount Everest. That was 1953. The first people to travel around the world by land visiting both poles started their journey in 1979 and finished in 1982. The last of these great events is the first solo hot air balloon flight round the World that was in 2002. The pilot was Steve Fossett.
YOUR TURN	Class or small group discussion to see which of these things students would like to do and why / why not.
2A	Focus on the text about the race for the South Pole. Students read the introduction. Then they read the text and fill the gaps using the information from the map. Check student answers **Key:** In 1911, there were two expeditions to the South Pole. One was Norwegian led by the famous explorer Roald Amundsen. It started from *the Bay of Whales* in *October 1911*. The second expedition, led by the British explorer Robert Scott started a month later in *November 1911* from *Cape Evans*. The two teams followed different routes. Amundsen reached the Transantarctic Mountains in *November 1911* and Scott reached the same mountains in *December 1911*. Amundsen reached the South Pole in *December 1911* and Scott arrived 33 days later in *January 1912*. Amundsen's successful expedition returned to base camp. Scott's mission was a disaster. All the members of the team died on the return journey. Scott himself died in *March 1912*.
2B	Comprehension check. **Key:** 1. *False*, 2. *False*, 3. *True*, 4. *False*.
OVER TO YOU	Students select the 7 things they would take with them on an expedition to the Antarctic. This should be a cooperative task. Students then compare their choices with that of another group. Encourage students to justify their choices.
Optional Extension	The activity in the **Over to You** could be extended with the teacher reducing the number of items to 5 after students have made their choice of 7.
Homework Option	Students write a biography of one of the famous explorers from the lesson.
Web links	www.bbc.co.uk/history/discovery/exploration The section of the BBC's website devoted to the history of exploration. www.antarctica.ac.uk The official UK Antarctic website. www.nasa.gov NASA's comprehensive site about space travel and much more.

THE CHILL ZONE 6

pp. 88-89

THE DOMESDAY GAME
Key: 1. *30 cows;* 2. *90 chickens;* 3. *20 ducks;* 4. *10 pigs;* 5. *38 sheep;* 6. *Legs = 532*
(120 cow legs, 180 chicken legs, 40 duck legs, 40 pig legs, 152 sheep legs)

Super Sudoku Craze
Key:

3	8	5	7	6	4	2	1	9
7	9	4	5	1	2	6	8	3
2	1	6	3	9	8	7	5	4
5	7	3	4	8	9	1	2	6
9	4	1	2	7	6	5	3	8
8	6	2	1	5	3	9	4	7
6	3	8	9	2	5	4	7	1
1	5	9	8	4	7	3	6	2
4	2	7	6	3	1	8	9	5

Morse Code
Key: *What is your name?*

The Hogwarts grades
Key: Pass: O = *outstanding*, E = *exceeds expectations*, A = *acceptable*. Fail: P = *poor*, D = *dreadful*, T = *troll*.

Swot spot
Key: 1. *c*, 2. *a*, 3. *b*.

WORKING WITH TEXTS 6

pp. 90-91

Entering the New World

This is the sixth long text in a section aimed at preparing students for state examinations. The texts are graded according to level and are progressive. Each text is followed by a series of comprehension questions and work on summary skills. **Note:** the reason for the highlighted areas of text becomes evident when students do the summary skills activity.

Before you read
1 This pre-reading activity is designed to get students thinking about the text before they start reading to help with orientation. **Tip:** this could be done as a whole group activity using board work.

Reading
2 Students read the text and answer the comprehension questions.
   Key:
   1. More than 20 million.
   2. To escape poverty at home.
   3. A new immigration station.
   4. Annie Moore.
   5. She was 15 years old.
   6. They had a quick medical check.
   7. Officials asked 29 questions to the immigrants.
   8. Because it gave the immigrant the right to stay in America.
   9. H meant the immigrant had a heart problem.
   10. A museum of immigration.

Summary skills
3A Students focus on the highlighted words in the first paragraph and on how they can be linked together to make a good summary.

3B Following the example, students do the same for paragraph 2.

3C Students can go on to summarize the whole text when their answers to 3b are effective.

47

SCHOOL LIFE AND EDUCATION LESSON **7A**

Public Schools Types of schools pp. 92-93

This lesson introduces the issue of public and state schools in the UK.

Objectives: students will...	• learn / revise the lexis of school facilities • learn about Roald Dahl's experience in public school by reading part of his autobiography • compare students' own system of schooling with others
Warm-up	Students think about the type of school they attend. **Culture note:** in British English, state schools are open to all and financed by the state, while public schools are high profile private schools. In the USA, public schools are financed by the state / individual states.
1	To reinforce the difference between various types of school, students use their dictionaries to find out which schools are private in the UK. **Key:** Private schools in the UK: *public school, boarding school, private school, prep school*. State schools: *state school, comprehensive school*.
2A	Focus the students' attention on the pictures of Eton to orient them. Students then match the questions to the answers. The gap-fill is not necessary at this stage. **Key:** 1. *C*, 2. *B*, 3. *A*, 4. *E*, 5. *F*, 6. *D*.
2B CD2 Track 8	Students listen for the missing information. Students should listen to the track twice, as happens in international examinations. **Audio script and key** (Accents: Eng) SALLY Hi James, thanks for talking to me about your school. JAMES No problem. SALLY Well then, how many students are there at your school? JAMES This year, there are about *1,300* students in the school. All *boys*. SALLY OK and do you have normal classes? JAMES Yes, the same as other schools. You know, *maths, chemistry*, English etc., but we can also do *Japanese* and Russian. SALLY Japanese. Great. How many students are there in a class? JAMES In the first couple of years there are usually *twenty to twenty-four* students in a class. Later, the classes get smaller. SALLY There are about 28 in mine! What about sports? What sports do you do? JAMES Some students play *rugby*, others do rowing or some play *tennis*. Actually there are lots of other sports to choose from like polo, sub-aqua and tai chi. I do tai chi. SALLY OK and do you have any special facilities? JAMES Well, there are lots of sports fields, *24* science laboratories and really good *music* facilities. Art and design studios are fantastic too. SALLY Wow. My last question then, are there any famous people who were past students? JAMES Yes, lots. Princes William and Harry recently. Then there were famous *writers* like Shelley, lots of famous politicians and fictional characters like *James Bond*! SALLY Thanks James. JAMES You're welcome!
YOUR TURN	Students answer the questions in 2A about their own school. Ideally, this should be a speaking activity.
Literature	The text is unsimplified and comes from Roald Dahl's autobiography. Roald Dahl (1916-90) was a British writer from a Norwegian family. He was most famous for his children's books such as Charlie and the Chocolate Factory (1964), James and the Giant Peach (1961 USA, 1967 UK), The BFG (1982).
3A CD2 Track 9	Students should read and listen to the extract from "Boy". At this stage, students should not be concerned about any new vocabulary in the text. For **audio script** see Student's Book page 93. (**Accent:** Eng)
3B	Ask the students to tick the food mentioned in the text. **Tip:** make sure that they are using the keywords and not blocking on the vocabulary they don't understand. For example, *cake* is the keyword and *currant* is unimportant. **Note:** the pictures are in four pairs. **Key:** *half a cake, a pot of strawberry jam, a couple of oranges, a bar of chocolate*.
3C	Students move on to the vocabulary exercise related to non-food treasures Dahl kept in his tuck-box. **Note:** the lexis is more complex here, so students will need help with some of the items. **Key**: *a catapult, a compass, six lead soldiers, a pocket-knife, a box of conjuring tricks, a magnet, a ball of string, some foreign stamps, two stink-bombs, a pet frog, a clockwork car*.
OVER TO YOU	Students make a list of 15 things they would keep in a tuck-box. Remind students that they will be away from home for two or three months. Students should then compare their work with that of another group.
Optional Extension	Students work on one of Roald Dahl's titles such as Charlie and the Chocolate Factory. Students who have seen the film could write a review for those who haven't. Students who haven't seen the film work on another popular film.
Homework Option	Students write a paragraph about their school, using the questions in 1a as a guideline.
Web links	www.etoncollege.com Eton's oficial website. www.sbsa.org.uk Association of UK secondary schools. www.ofsted.gov.uk The UK government's school's inspections website.

48

PEOPLE AND LIFESTYLES LESSON **7B**

Life Then and Life Now
Daily life in the past and today   pp. 94-95

This lesson addresses the types of homes which can be found in the ESW.

Objectives: students will...	• learn / revise the lexis of household objects • learn / revise the lexis of TV sets • learn about product design • compare life in the recent past with life today • discuss homes of the future
Warm-up	Students calculate how old they would be if they were born in 1950.
1A	Students mark the household items on the picture. They should know most of the vocabulary, but some help will be necessary.
1B 1C CD2 Track 10	Students circle the ten things which didn't exist in the 1950s. They then listen and check their answers. **Key:** *DVD Player, microwave, remote control, cans, computer, MP3 player, videogame console, dishwasher, cordless phone, digital clock.* **Note:** cans did exist but not drinks cans. Obviously, clocks existed, but digital ones had not yet been invented. Similarly, the cordless phone was not yet available. Computers existed in the 1950s, but they were so big they needed a large room to themselves! **Audio script** (Accent: GB) In the 1950s house, there were no computers of course. Entertainment was very different. We didn't have DVDs or MP3 players. We had the radio and some families had a television. Televisions didn't have a remote control… er… let me think….We didn't have videogames of course. I had a fantastic record player – I just loved my record player. We had the telephone in the living room. Er… there were no cordless phones in the 1950s. In the kitchen we had a washing machine and we had a large fridge, but we didn't have a dishwasher. Of course, we didn't have microwaves at all. There must be some more things. Oh yes, we didn't have digital clocks, our clocks were all analogue. And, a strange thing: there were no cans for soft drinks. All the drinks came in bottles!
2A	This text is the extract from a diary from 1955. It contains a number of items which are impossible because they are anachronistic. Students circle the incorrect information. There are a number of distractors in the text and seven impossible items. **Key:** *Men landing on the Moon (1969); email wasn't invented; the Euro didn't exist; there were no mobile phones for texting; there was no newspaper recycling; the Beatles weren't recording yet; it wasn't possible to surf the net.*
2B	Students check with their partners.
YOUR TURN	Students make a list of things they did yesterday and decide which of these were possible in the 1950s.
3A	Ask students to look at the pictures and decide which TV is the oldest.
3B	Now students read the text and use the information to match them to the pictures. For **audio script**, see Student's Book page 93. **Key:** *1. C, 2. D, 3. A, 4. B.*
3C	Check the students' comprehension of the text with the True or False exercise. **Key:** *1. False (All TVs were black and white), 2. False (in the early 1980s there were only 4 channels), 3. True, 4. True.*
3D WEB PROJECT	This is a web project where students find illustrations from the Internet to show how the design of familiar objects has changed over the years. They then write a description of how it has changed.
OVER TO YOU	Students work together to look at designing a high-tech house for the future. **Tip:** encourage them to think about automation. They then describe their house to another pair.
Optional Extension	Students could work on a house in the Victorian era to see what people didn't have.
Homework Option	Encourage students to talk to their older relatives about differences in life then and now and then write a short report showing the differences.
Web links	www.bbc.co.uk The official BBC website. www.moma.org The Museum of Modern Art in New York which has a famous design section. www.designmuseum.org A museum dedicated to product design.

SPORT & LEISURE

Going for Gold! Sporting heroes

LESSON **7C**

pp. 96-97

This lesson introduces the subject of the Olympic Games via those held in the ESW in London 1908, Sydney 2000 and those to be held again in London in 2012.

Objectives: students will...	• learn / revise the lexis of sports vocabulary • learn / revise the lexis of competitive sport • learn about the Olympic ideal • compare the Olympics in the past with those in the present • prepare a talk about sport
Warm-up	Students look at the flag and discuss the meaning of the rings. **Key:** *Many sources say that the rings on the flag originally represented the five inhabited continents (the Americas were regarded as one). Others disagree. All sources appear to agree that the five colours of the rings and the white background show the universality of the Olympics since every national flag in the world contains at least one of these six colours.*
1A	Students read the text and complete the table. **Key:** |	London 1908	Sydney 2000
---	---	---
Number of countries	22	199
Number of athletes (men)	1,971	6,582
Number of athletes (women)	37	4,069
Number of events	110	300
New sport for this Games	Ice-skating	Taekwondo
Fastest men's time at 100m	10.8 seconds	9.87 seconds
Country with the most medals	USA (35)	USA (97)
Best individual performances	Henry Taylor (GB) Mel Shepherd (USA)	Marion Jones (USA)	
1B	Students compare the things which have changed since 1908. E.g. there are more sports today, men can run faster today, there are more athletes today, there are many more women athletes today, America still wins the most medals.
2A	Warm students up for this activity by looking at the picture of Amo, an Olympic hopeful canoeist. Students imagine that they are reporters and use the words from the prompts to write questions to ask Amo about her life.
2B CD2 Track 11	Students listen to the text the first time to see if the journalist asks their questions. On the second listening, students listen for the answers. Although students' questions may be different from those asked in the audio script, this represents a good opportunity for students to have the freedom to use their imaginations as interviewers. **Audio script and key** (Accents: Eng) INT. Hello Amo. You are hoping to be an athlete in the 2012 Olympics in London is that right? AMO Yes, that's right. I'm a canoeist. INT. Can you tell us about your day? *When do you train?* AMO Well, I get up at about 5.30 in the morning, every day including the weekend. I train very hard. Usually I go to the gym before school. I go canoeing after school and on Saturdays and Sundays. INT. You work very hard. *Do you have to eat special food?* AMO No, I eat the same food as my friends. I eat a lot though, especially a lot of pasta. INT. *Do you like canoeing or is it like a job?* AMO I love it. I really like it when it's raining, when it's sunny, even when it's snowing!! INT. *Is it a difficult sport?* AMO It depends. If you want to do it for fun, just go to your local club – it's easy. If you want to go to the 2012 Olympics, it's difficult, of course!! INT. Good luck Amo!
OVER TO YOU	Students prepare a short talk to give to the class about a sport they like. **Note:** this type of activity is good preparation for the Trinity Examinations. If you have a large class, students could give their talks in groups of six or seven. Ask students to make notes while they are listening to others.
Optional Extension	Students write about one of their Olympic heroes. This could be a person from the past or a current sports hero.
Homework Option	Students write about a sport they would like to do at the Olympics.
Web links	www.olympics.org.uk The UK arm of the official Olympic website with information about 2012 London Olympics. www.specialolympics.org The international site for the Olympic Games for people with learning difficulties. www.olympic.org The International Olympic Committee's official website. Some pages are in French.

HISTORY AND TRADITIONS LESSON **7D**

The Age of Discovery — 1492 and beyond — pp. 98-99

This lesson addresses the discovery of America and Australia and the concept of navigating without modern instruments.

Objectives: students will...	• learn / revise the lexis of travelling by sea • learn about Columbus and Cook • learn how to make a quadrant to measure latitude • learn how to use a quadrant
Warm-up	Students brainstorm all they know about Magellan, Vespucci and Columbus. **Culture note:** Ferdinand Magellan /məˈgelən/ was Portuguese but under the command of Spain. His mission was the first to complete a circumnavigation of the world in 1522, although Magellan himself had been killed. Amerigo Vespucci (1451-1512) was an Italian merchant and navigator. He made at least two voyages to the New World. The word America is said to come from his first name. Christopher Columbus (1451-1506) was born in Italy, but served the Spanish. His 1492 mission discovered the New World.
1A 1B CD2 Track 12	Focus students' attention on the map. They should be able to complete the text simply by observing the details on it. Students then listen to check their answers. **Audio script and key** (**Accent:** GB): Christopher Columbus sailed from *Palos de la Frontera* in August 1492. His intention was to find a new route to Asia. He also wanted to prove that the world was round so he went west. He had *three* ships and 88 men. He stopped at the *Canary Islands*. He then continued west. On the 12th of October, Columbus landed in the *Bahamas*. Then he sailed around the Caribbean and visited *Cuba*. At Christmas 1492, Columbus established a colony called La Navidad on the island of *Haiti*. He returned to *Spain* in early 1493. He was a hero! He believed that the new lands were in Asia – he called them the *West Indies*. **Language note:** in spoken British English we usually say 'the' and 'of' when giving a date. These are not usually written.
YOUR TURN	**A** Students guess which of the four things navigators brought back from the New World **Key:** *tomatoes, sweetcorn, chocolate and tobacco.* **B** Students guess which of the four things navigators took to the New World. **Key:** *rice, diseases, olives, wheat.* **C** Check students' answers.
2A CD2 Track 13	Ask students to look at the text about James Cook. Students read and listen and circle the correct answer. For **audio script** see Student's Book page 99. (**Accent:** Eng) **Key:** *shop, maths, astronomy, 1769, Australia, New Zealand, Hawaii.*
2B	Students list the places he visited from the text. They then put the list in alphabetical order as fast as possible. This is to improve reference and dictionary skills. **Key:** *Australia, Hawaii, Newfoundland, New Zealand.*
OVER TO YOU	You need **photocopies of the quadrant** from page 78 of this Teacher's Book to give to the students. Students also need glue, cardboard, string and a bead to act as a weight. Full instructions for making the quadrant are in the Student's Book. To use their quadrants, students will have to cut out some stars and place them high on the classroom wall or ceiling. Full instructions for using the quadrant are in the Student's Book.
Optional Extension	Students research a British explorer such as Sir Francis Drake.
Homework Option	Students write about what Columbus brought back from America and what he took there, joining up the ideas from exercise 1.
Web links	www.nmm.ac.uk The official website of the National Maritime Museum, UK. www.heritage.nf.ca Newfoundland heritage site with information about Captain Cook. www.columbusnavigation.com Information about navigation techniques in the age of Columbus.

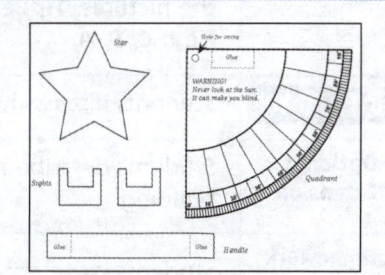

THE WORLD WE LIVE IN

LESSON 7E

Great Buildings — Manmade wonders and manmade mistakes

pp. 100-101

This lesson explores buildings from the ESW such as the London Eye and the Empire State Building.
Tip: students may be interested to follow the building of the Freedom Tower, the construction of which is taking place at Ground Zero in New York.

Objectives: students will...	• learn / revise the lexis of height and weight and parts of a building • learn / revise "how" questions • learn about manmade construction disasters • discuss beautiful buildings
Warm-up	Students brainstorm famous buildings in the ESW. These could be *Sydney Opera House, Big Ben, Buckingham Palace, the Empire State Building* etc.
1A	Students read the information on the page and answer the questions. Focus on the question forms. **Key:** 1. *135 m*; 2. *10 tonnes*; 3. *¼ of normal walking speed*; 4. *more than 40 km*; 5. *a week*; 6. *25 passengers*; 7. *1,700 tonnes*.
2A	Focus students' attention on the short text about the Empire State Building. Then ask them to try to guess the answers to the questions. This is a pre-listening activity to familiarize students with the text.
2B CD2 Track 14	Students listen to this tour guide giving information about the Empire State Building. Students should listen to the track twice, as happens in international examinations. Check students' answers. **Note:** some sources say that there are 103 floors in the Empire State Building although the majority say there are 102. This is possibly because the ground floor in the UK is called the first floor in the USA, the first floor in the UK is called the second floor in the USA and so on. **Language notes:** 'elevator' is American English, 'lift' is British English; in American English the numbering system is slightly different from the British: the "and" in large numbers is omitted. e.g. one hundred **and** two in BrE becomes one hundred two in AmE. All the numbers in this text are in American English. **Audio script and key** (Accents: USA) GUIDE Hello everyone, welcome to the Empire State Building. When it was built in 1930, the Empire State Building was the tallest building in the world. *It's 443 m high.* VISITOR 1 How many floors are there? GUIDE Well there are *102 floors in total*. And this means that there are a lot of steps. In fact there are *1,860 steps* in the building! VISITOR 2 Wow, I hope there's an elevator! GUIDE Don't worry. In fact, there are *73 elevators* in total, so you don't have to walk up the 1,860 steps. VISITOR 2 How fast are the elevators? GUIDE It's possible to go from the lobby to the 80th floor in 45 seconds. VISITOR 2 Wow! Incredible! GUIDE Another interesting fact is that there are *6,500 windows* in the building. VISITOR 1 6,500! That's a lot of windows to clean! GUIDE Right. Shall we go inside?
3	This part of the lesson focuses on some engineering disasters. Students must match the text to the pictures. **Tip:** encourage them to explain the problems in their own words. **Key:** C, B, A.
OVER TO YOU	Students discuss the buildings they like and don't like in their town or in their country.
Optional Extension	Students describe a public building in their town such as a theatre, the town hall or any historic building.
Homework Option	Students write about one of the most important tourist attractions in their country's capital.
Web links	www.esbnyc.com The official website of the Empire State Building in New York. www.londoneye.com Lots of fun facts and figures about the world's biggest observation wheel.

52

THE CHILL ZONE 7

pp. 102-103

"The Columbus Rap"

CD2 Track 15 Audio script and key:

In fourteen hundred and ninety-two
Columbus sailed the ocean blue.

He had three ships and left from Spain;
He sailed through sunshine, wind and rain.

He sailed by night; he sailed by day
He used the stars to find his way.

Day after day they looked for land;
They dreamed of trees and rocks and sand.

October 12 their dream came true,
You never saw a happier crew!

ELECTRICWORD
Key: Across: 3. *fridge*, 4. *dishwasher*, 5. *player*, 6. *control*, 7. *television*.
Down: 1. *console*, 2. *microwave*, 5. *player*.

Swot spot
Key: 1. *a*, 2. *b*, 3. *c*, 4. *a*.

TUCK BOX
Key: *J* on the bottom line

Experiment
Culture note: lots of people didn't wash in cold water in the morning, but many did!

CONSTRUCTIONS
Key: 1. *skyscraper*, 2. *bridge*, 3. *elevator*, 4. *wheel*.

WORKING WITH TEXTS 6

pp. 104-105

In and around London
This is the seventh long text in a section aimed at preparing students for state examinations. The texts are graded according to level and are progressive. Each text is followed by a comprehension activity and work on summary skills.

Before you read
1 Students list the most famous buildings in their capital city.

Reading
2 Students read the guide book extracts and answer the questions.
Key:
1. *A terrible fire*; 2. *A bell*; 3. *450*; 4. *The changing of the guard*; 5. *A famous general from the First World War*; 6. *1066*; 7. *A collection of arms and weapons*; 8. *90 seconds*; 9. *At Piccadilly Circus*; 10. *Admiral Nelson's*.

Summary skills
3A This activity looks at various synonyms.
Key: 1. *tower*, 2. *modern*, 3. *police*, 4. *jewels*.
3B Students underline the key information in each paragraph and then summarize each paragraph.

SCHOOL LIFE AND EDUCATION   LESSON **8A**

Home Education   Unusual education   pp. 106-107

This lesson explores the issue of home education. This is a common concept in many parts of the ESW for reasons of distance or sometimes ideology. A typical chemistry lesson from home education study takes up the second part of the lesson.

Objectives: students will...	• learn / revise the lexis of acids and alkalis • recognize hazard symbols • learn about the School of the Air • design a hazard warning symbol • compare lifestyles of students and those educated at home
Warm-up	Build up a list of things the students like and don't like about school on the board.
1A	**Tip:** encourage students to look at the headline and picture in order to predict the content of the text.
1B	Students skim-read the text to find out the content. **Note:** this should take no longer than a minute and serves to do some training into approaching texts.
1C	Now students read the text carefully and answer the True / False / Doesn't say questions. **Key:** 1. *False*, 2. *True*, 3. *True*, 4. *Doesn't say*, 5. *True*, 6. *False*.
2A	Students read the introductory text about the USA and the UK. Samantha comes from Scotland.
2B CD2 Track 16	Give students a few moments to read through the questions. Students listen to the interview with Samantha and answer the questions. Students should listen to the track twice, as happens in international examinations. **Key:** 1. *A*, 2. *C*, 3. *A*, 4. *B*, 5. *A*, 6. *A*. **Audio script** (**Accents:** Int. = Eng, Samantha = Scot.) INT. Do you like Home Education? SAMANTHA Yes I really enjoy it. My parents are both good teachers. INT. What's your best subject? SAMANTHA I don't like English very much, I like science. But my best subject is definitely maths. INT. What material do you use? SAMANTHA I have ordinary school books. Then I also use DVDs and the computer, I use the Internet a lot for my lessons. INT. How many hours a week do you study? SAMANTHA I do from nine to twelve o'clock every day except Saturday and Sunday. Then from 4 to 5 in the afternoon. That's 4 hours a day for 5 days. 20 hours a week. Yes the total is 20 hours a week. INT. You don't have any school friends. Are you lonely? SAMANTHA No, I have lots of friends. I go to dance classes on Tuesdays and Thursdays! I'm also in a swimming team. INT. What's good about home education? SAMANTHA My lessons are specially for me. Then, of course, I don't have homework!!! And I can study in my pyjamas!
YOUR TURN	Students talk about the advantages and disadvantages of studying at home.
3A	Students match the danger signs to the words. **Key:** *corrosive, explosive, flammable, irritant, poisonous.*
3B CD2 Track 17	Students listen to an extract from a School of the Air lesson on chemistry and complete the pH scale. **Audio script and key** (**Accent:** Aus) The pH scale goes from pH number 1 to pH number 14. On your diagram, red is the colour of *strong acids*. Green is the colour of *neutral*. Neutral is pH number 7. Dark blue is the colour of *strong alkalis*. Today, we're going to examine...
3C	Students look at the pH of common household items and answer the questions. **Note:** they will need help with some vocabulary items. **Key:** 1. a) *any acid from 1-6 on the scale*, b) *any alkali from 8-14 on the scale*, c) *pure water is the neutral substance*; 2. *irritants*; 3. *lemon juice*; 4. *bleach*.
OVER TO YOU	Students design their own hazard warning sign for homework, a test or an angry teacher. They can do this using the **photocopy of the worksheet** on page 79 of this Teacher's Book **(Part 2 – Hazard warnings)**.
Optional Extensions	• Students write a letter to Samantha explaining what they do on an average school day. • **Photocopiable worksheet** on page 79 of this Teacher's Book. **Note:** for part one you will need to provide universal indicator paper and choose non-hazardous products for the students to test. Students test their products and complete the chart. Part two relates to the **Over to You** section in this lesson.
Homework Option	Students look out for warning symbols for a week and make a note of where they saw them.
Web links	www.cyberheritage.com/schooloftheair Information about the Australian School of the Air. www.miamisci.org The Miami Museum of Science and Planetarium's official website.

PEOPLE AND LIFESTYLES LESSON **8B**

Town and Country
Village, small town and city life   pp. 108-109

This lesson explores the contrast between town and country life.

Objectives: students will...	• learn / revise the lexis of towns and the countryside • learn about living in a tourist location • compare city and country life • plan a day trip to a big city on a budget • write a postcard about the trip
Warm-up	Students put these places in order of size. **Key:** 1. *metropolis (the biggest)*, 2. *city*, 3. *town*, 4. *small town*, 5. *village*. **Tip:** encourage the students to give examples of each from their area.
1	Students read the texts and complete the tables with the good things about New York and Kaycee, Wyoming, USA. **Language note:** horseback riding = AmE, horse-riding = BrE. **Key:** Good things about New York: *great stores, good museums, Central Park is neat with lots to do (skateboarding / ice-skating), it's good for cinema and theatre, it's good for music, there's a good baseball team.* Good things about Kaycee: *it's quiet, safe, there's a lot of space, no traffic problems, it's near a city for shopping, horseback riding, canoeing, Yellowstone is nearby for camping and trekking, there's a rodeo.*
2 CD2 Track 18	This introduces the negative points of living in a tourist destination. **Tip:** if your school is in a tourist area, you could elicit the negative points before doing the activity. Give students a few moments to read through the comments and check vocabulary. Students listen to Angus and Karen talking about the things they don't like about Bourton-on-the-Water and Yulara. Students should listen to each track twice, as happens in international examinations. **Key:** Angus: *It's boring; There isn't a cinema; There aren't many young people; There are too many tourists; It takes a long time to get to school.* Karen: *It's boring; There aren't many young people; There aren't many shops in the village; There are too many tourists.* **Audio script** (**Accents:** Angus = Eng, Karen = Aus.) ANGUS I really hate living here. It's really, really boring. There isn't a cinema...well, there isn't <u>anything</u> to do in the evenings. That's because there are no young people. Bourton-on-the-Water is really pretty. It's a beautiful village. This means we have too many tourists in the summer. It's terrible in the summer, just too many tourists. Another thing I don't like is that I go to school in Cheltenham. That's about 25 km away and I go on the bus so it takes hours. KAREN I hate living in Yulara. It's really very boring. There isn't anything to do. There really isn't anything to do. There are no young people - everybody is over 50. Well not everybody but most people. Shopping is impossible. There are only one or two shops and they're for tourists, not residents. It takes a long time to go shopping. Sometimes there are too many tourists too.
YOUR TURN	Students discuss tourist places they know. **Tip:** encourage them to consider how the places change between summer and winter.
OVER TO YOU	Students work together to plan a trip to a big city. **A** They must agree on which five things to take with them. **B** Now students must agree on four activities to do on the day trip. Remind them that they only have £25 to spend. **C** Students calculate how much money they have left. **D** Students write a postcard to their friend in a KET-style activity.
Optional Extension	Students write up a plan of their day trip using the 'going to' future.
Homework Option	Students write about the good points of the place where they live.
Web links	www.nyhallsci.org The New York Hall of Science – the museum website. www.kayceewyoming.org Further information about Kaycee. www.the-cotswolds.org Tourist information about the Cotswolds.

55

SPORT & LEISURE LESSON 8C

It won 8 Oscars! Cinema   pp. 110-111

This lesson explores both western and Indian cinema and gives the students the opportunity to give their own Oscar-style awards.

Objectives: students will...	• learn / revise the lexis of film genres • learn / revise the lexis of cinema jobs • learn about Bollywood and Indian cinema	• compare Hollywood and Bollywood • discuss their favourite films • give awards to people in the class
Warm-up	Discuss students' cinema-going habits as a whole class activity.	
1A	Students match the film still to the genre. **Key:** *horror, western, sci-fi, rom-com.*	
1B CD2 Track 19	Play the soundtrack and ask the students to match the track to the film. **Key:** 1. *western*, 2. *rom-com*, 3. *horror*, 4. *sci-fi.* **Language note:** rom-com is a widely-used term for romantic comedy **Pronunciation note**: sci-fi /saɪ faɪ/	
1C	Students discuss the films they like best from the genre list. **Language note:** bio-pics are biographical films.	
2A 2B CD2 Track 20	Encourage students to guess the answers to the questions about the Oscar statuettes. Students then listen and check. **Key:** 1. *B*, 2. *A*, 3. *B*, 4. *A*, 5. *B*, 6. *C.* **Audio script** (Accents: USA) Q: What are Oscars made of? A: They're made of metal. Gold-plated metal. Q: And how tall is an Oscar? A: It's 13 and a half inches, that's 34.29 cm. Q: How much does an Oscar weigh? A: Each one weighs 8 and a half pounds which is 3.86 kg. Q: How many people does it take to make an Oscar? A: There are 12 people involved in making an Oscar. Q: And how long does it take to make one? A: It's a long process. It takes about 20 hours. Q: And finally, how many Oscars are made each year? A: The number is usually somewhere between fifty and sixty.	
2C	Students work in pairs to think about their favourite films and give academy awards.	
3	Students read the information about Bollywood and Hollywood and tick the True / False boxes. Point out the information about Kishan Shrikanth in the **Incredible but true!!** box. **Key:** 1. *True*, 2. *False*, 3. *True*, 4. *True*, 5. *True*, 6. *False.*	
YOUR TURN	Students discuss what they usually eat when they go to the cinema and compare this with the USA.	
OVER TO YOU	This is an opportunity to give awards to other students in the group based on their talents.	
Optional Extension	Students write a scene dialogue from a film they know well. They could then act these dialogues out in front of the class.	
Homework Option	Write a review of the last film seen at the cinema or on TV. Suggest that students divide up their review into plot, characters and opinion.	
Web links	www.bollywoodpremiere.com Everything you ever wanted to know about Bollywood and its stars. www.oscars.org The official website of the Academy of Motion Picture Arts and Sciences. www.hollywoodusa.co.uk Lots of information about the lives of Hollywood stars and the place itself.	

HISTORY AND TRADITIONS
LESSON 8D

"I have a dream..." Civil and Human Rights
pp. 112-113

This lesson explores the issue of civil rights and racism via the biographies of Dr. Martin Luther King Jr. and Nelson Mandela.

Objectives: students will...	• learn / revise the language of biographical information • learn about civil rights for African-Americans and South Africans • compare their dreams for the future • do research into the Suffragettes or Mahatma Gandhi
Warm-up CD2 Track 21	Students listen to the extract from Martin Luther King's famous speech in Washington in 1963. The full text of the speech is available with an audio track at www.thekingcenter.org. Some students may know who said this, encourage them to say. For **audio script** see Student's Book page 112. (**Accent**: USA)
1A	Students look at the two fact-files about Martin Luther King and Nelson Mandela. They put the missing information into the correct place. **Key:** MLK fact-file: Place of birth: *Atlanta*; From 1957 to 1968 he travelled *over 6 million miles*; *He was assassinated* in 1968. NM fact-file: Place of birth: *Umata, South Africa*; He joined the *African National Congress*; He *left prison* in 1990.
1B	Students read the text about racism in America and the USA.
1C	Point out to students that the answers to the comprehension questions are in the fact-files as well as the texts. **Key:** 1. *American and South African*; 2. *Martin Luther King*; 3. Choose from: *vote, use same entrance in cinemas, sit together on buses, eat in "white" restaurants, walk down the street with white people*; 4. *No*; 5. *Nelson Mandela*; 6. *He won the Nobel Peace Prize*; 7. *Martin Luther King*; 8. *Nelson Mandela*; 9. *He was assassinated*; 10. *For equality for blacks and whites*.
1D	Discuss whether your town has a street, square or building named after one of these men. **Tip:** you could discuss other people who have streets named after them and why this is the case.
WEB PROJECT	This is a web project to allow students to find out more about either Mahatma Gandhi or the Suffragettes.
OVER TO YOU	Students discuss their dreams for the future.
Optional Extension	If your class is mature enough, you could lead a discussion on racism in your own country.
Homework Option	Students write a speech about their dreams for the future.
Web links	www.nobelprize.org Information about Nobel Peace Prize winners. www.thekingcenter.org About Martin Luther King. www.nelsonmandela.org The Nelson Mandela foundation.

THE WORLD WE LIVE IN LESSON **8E**

London Old and New
Dickens' London and London today pp. 114-115

This lesson explores the issue of London in the time of Charles Dickens.

Objectives: students will...	• learn / revise the lexis of city dangers in the past • learn / revise adjectives describing fog • learn about hardships in Victorian London • compare London today with London in the past • discuss what they can do to clean up their town
Warm-up	A quick quiz about London. This should be rapid fire and a whole class activity. **Key:** 1. Some possible buildings are: *The Houses of Parliament, Westminster Abbey, Buckingham Palace, The Tower of London, Tower Bridge*. These are also found in the **Working with Texts**, **7** (pages 104-105). 2. Some possible London football teams are *Arsenal, Chelsea, Spurs (Tottenham Hotspur), West Ham United, Fulham, Crystal Palace, Queens Park Rangers, Millwall*. 3. *The River Thames*. **Pronunciation note**: /temz/
1A	Check that the students understand the vocabulary. Students label the street scenes. **Key:** From left to right *pickpockets, child labour, prison, the Workhouse, the smell, pestilence, fog, the river*.
1B	Ask students to look up the meaning of these words in their dictionaries or explain them yourself to the students.
1C CD2 Track 22	Students read and listen to the text from the opening of Charles Dickens' Bleak House. This text has been simplified from the original. For **audio script** see Student's Book page 115. (**Accent:** Eng)
YOUR TURN	Students write their own description of a foggy day.
2A CD2 Track 23	This is a listening activity. Point out that London today does not suffer from fog as it did in the past and that it is now much cleaner than it was. Give students a few moments to look at the pictures. On the first listening they should tick the pictures related to what the specialist says. **Key:** *salmon, seals, tufted ducks, whales*. For **audio script** see exercise 2B below.
2B CD2 Track 24	On the second listening, students answer the questions. **Key:** 1. *No*; 2. *No*. **Audio script** (**Accent:** GB) The River Thames in London is much cleaner today. There aren't any really big problems for animals and fish. We often see salmon in the river in modern London. This means that the water is very clean. Salmon need very clean water to live. In the last few years, people have seen a lot of seals in the river in the centre of the city. This shows that the water is much cleaner than in Dickens' time. There are also some rare ducks, like the tufted duck for example and we have even had a whale in the Thames recently. The whale was outside the Houses of Parliament. Whales don't live in the Thames though.
OVER TO YOU	Students work in pairs to plan a clean-up of their town.
Optional Extension	Students work online or use encyclopaedias to compile a biography of Charles Dickens.
Homework Option	Students imagine that they live in London in the 1850s. They write a description of the town.
Web links	www.tfl.gov.uk The transport for London website. www.the-river-thames.co.uk A personal view of the River Thames. www.portoflondon.co.uk Official website of the Port of London Authority with information about events, the environment etc.

THE CHILL ZONE 8

pp. 116-117

Swot spot
Key: 1. *river*; 2. *prison*; 3. *smell*; 4. *smog*; 5. *dirty*; 6. *pickpocket*.

Wordsearch:

```
B O L L Y W O O D E
X P T H R I L L E R
C I N A A C T O R J
P S P E C I A L F X
O O A T R O S C A R
C I N E M A T A N K
H O R R O R F I L M
M O P A C T R E S S
Z D I R E C T O R Y
S O U N D T R A C K
```

Key: The missing word is *Oscar*.

WORKING WITH TEXTS 8

pp. 118-119

Universal Studios Tour
This is the eighth long text in a section aimed at preparing students for state examinations. The texts are graded according to level and are progressive. Each text is followed by a comprehension activity and work on summary skills.

Before you read
1 Students use a translation dictionary to find the meanings of the words.

Reading
2 Students read the text and answer the questions.
Key:
1. *Hollywood*; 2. *Into the film and sound studios*; 3. *Films, music videos, advertisements and TV programmes*; 4. *By tram*; 5. *45 minutes*; 6. *Car stunts / collapsing bridges*; 7. *A Wild West town and New York City*; 8. *Desperate Housewives / CSI*; 9. *An earthquake, a flood, fog*; 10. *The War of the Worlds*.

Summary skills
3 Students summarize the text in a short paragraph. **Note:** this is the first complete summary students have been asked to tackle without extra help or guidance.

59

SCHOOL LIFE AND EDUCATION **LESSON 9A**

My English Class
Learning English around the world pp. 120-121

This lesson explores different ways of learning English around the world, from a year out to holiday courses.

Objectives: students will...	• learn / revise the lexis of activity courses • revise question forms • learn about studying abroad	• compare different ways of learning English • write an entry to a competition

Warm-up	Students discuss where they would like to go to study English.
1A	Make sure that students understand that Silvia is not American, but that she went to America to improve her English and live in a different culture for a year. In the first part of this exercise, students write the questions which would elicit these responses. More than one question may be correct. **Key - possible answers:** 1. *Where did you go? Where in America did you go to study English?* 2. *What did you study at school?* 3. *Where did you live? Who did you live with?* 4. *How many people were there in the family? Who did you live with?* 5. *Did you have a good time? Was it a good experience? Did you enjoy yourself?* 6. *What did you miss about home? Did you miss anything?*
1B CD2 Track 25	Students listen to see if their questions were the same. Students do not need to change their questions. **Audio script and key** (**Accents:** Int. = Eng, Silvia = Italian + USA.) INT. *Where in America did you go to study English?* SILVIA *I went to a High School in Cleveland, Ohio.* INT. *What did you study at school?* SILVIA *We studied all the usual things: math, science, English. A new subject for me was mechanics. It was cool.* INT. *Where did you live?* SILVIA *I lived near the school with an American family.* INT. *How many people were there in the family?* SILVIA *There were four in the family. Me, my host brother, my host Mom and my host Dad.* INT. *Did you have a good time?* SILVIA *Yes, I had a fantastic year. I loved school and I loved the family. I did lots of new things like camping and voluntary work.* INT. *What did you miss about home?* SILVIA *I really missed my family at first. I missed my cat too!*
YOUR TURN	Students discuss what they would miss about home.
2A	**Tip:** ask students whether they have ever been on a study holiday. Encourage students who have to to talk about their experiences. Then focus attention on the advertisements for English courses. Students answer the questions. **Key:** 1. *Rocky Mountain Activity School;* 2. *Rocky Mountain Activity School;* 3. *Rocky Mountain Activity School;* 4. *Tralee English Centre;* 5. *Tralee English Centre;* 6. *Rocky Mountain Activity School.*
2B CD2 Track 26	Give students a few moments to read through the radio advertisement. Students listen for the missing information. Students should listen to the track twice, as happens in international examinations. **Audio script and key** (**Accent:** NZ) Come and study English at The New Zealand English and Activity Centre English and fun! You learn English in the mornings from *9.30* to *12.30*. So that's for three hours. In the afternoons you can choose to go Kayaking, *windsurfing* or diving if you like sport. If you don't want to do sport you can do *photography* or cooking in the afternoons. You stay with great local families. The cost per week is only *200* New Zealand dollars. For more information contact Mrs. *Buckley.* That's B U C K L E Y on 855 8557572 See you there!
YOUR TURN	Students discuss which school they would prefer and why.
OVER TO YOU	This is a competition entry which mirrors the type of activity students are asked to do in the KET writing section. Encourage students to think why they would like to go to one of the language schools.
Optional Extension	Students write a radio advertisement for one of the other schools in exercise 2. If your school has a language laboratory, students could record their radio advertisement.
Homework Option	Students write a short email to one of the schools asking for a brochure and price list.
Web links	www.learnenglish.org.uk The British Council link to learning and teaching English. www.capls.com The Canadian Association of private language schools. www.tralee.ie Information about the city of Tralee.

60

PEOPLE AND LIFESTYLES
LESSON 9B
ESW Religions — Religion and worship
pp. 122–123

This lesson introduces the topic of religions and worship.

Objectives: students will…	• learn / revise the lexis of religious buildings • learn / revise the names of the different major faiths • learn about Australian Aboriginal Dreamtime stories • compare different places of worship • discuss stories and fables
Warm-up	Students look at the two pictures and try to guess which country these two places of worship are in. **Key:** *They are both in the UK.*
1	Students match the symbol to the place of worship. **Key:** *D, B, E, F, A, C.*
2A	Point out to students that the UK is a multicultural, multi-faith society. Students then transfer the information from the table to the pie chart. **Key:** The completed chart reads clockwise from the blue block: *Christian, Atheist, Agnostic, Muslim, Hindu, Sikh, Jewish, Buddhist, Other.*
2B	Students answer the comprehension questions. **Key:** 1. *True*, 2. *False*, 3. *True*, 4. *True*.
YOUR TURN	Discuss the major religions found in your country.
3A 3B CD2 Track 27	Students read the introduction about the Dreaming or Dreamtime. They then read a traditional story from the Dreaming. Students return the story to a logical order. They then listen to the story and check their order. **Culture note:** the fish in question is the bony bream. It is so full of bones that it is inedible. **Audio script and key** (Accent: Aus) A long time ago there was a group of Aboriginal people. They were very hungry. Three men from the group went fishing. They caught so many beautiful fish that the boat almost sank. They were very happy and they decided to go home. On the way home, they met an old man. They quickly covered the fish to hide it. The old man said, "I'm hungry. Did you catch any fish?" The three fishermen lied. They said, "We don't have enough fish for our people". The old man walked away saying, "You will never enjoy fish again". The fishermen went home. The people were very happy to see so many beautiful fish. They cooked all the fish on the fire. They started to eat the fish, but the fish were full of bones. It was impossible to eat them. The leader of the group didn't understand why the fish were so horrible. He asked, "Did you meet anyone on the road?" "Yes," said the fishermen, "An old man". "You stupid fishermen", said the leader. "That wasn't an old man. That was Ngurunderi. Ngurunderi made the fish full of bones, because you didn't share them. We can never eat this type of fish again."
3C	Students discuss the moral of the story.
OVER TO YOU	**A** Students work together to construct a story or fable. This could be one from their own faith or a popular legend or one of Aesop's fables. **B** See optional extension.
Optional Extension	Storytelling is also a very important aspect of Native American faith and customs. Students can read Native American stories from the website www.hanksville.org/storytellers.
Homework Option	Students describe a place of worship they know well.
Web links	www.aboriginalart.com.au The Australian Aboriginal Art and Culture Centre. www.didjshop.com/stories Students can get many more stories from the Dreamtime and see Aboriginal art. www.allblacks.com Has information about the Haka, the Maori chant. **Note:** the Haka from the **Did You Know?** on page 123 is also in **Chill Zone 9**, page 131, including the audio.

SPORT & LEISURE

LESSON 9C

Fashion — What's cool and what's not cool
pp. 124-125

This lesson introduces the concept of what's fashionable and unfashionable.

Objectives: students will...	• learn / revise the lexis of clothes and accessories • learn / revise the lexis of jewellery • learn about wristbands and campaigns • compare trendy and unfashionable things • design a wristband for a good cause
Warm-up CD2 Track 28	Students listen to the various ringtones and decide whether they are cool or uncool. **Audio script** 1. animal ringtone, 2. classical music, 3. jazz, 4. modern music, 5. non-polyphonic ringtone.
1	Students look at the photos and group the items into two lists, what's cool and what's uncool. **Culture note:** You may like to tell students that "kool" and "unkool" spelt with a K are typical of teen magazine slang. Often such magazines play with the spelling of words to make them more appealing to young people. **Tip:** encourage the students to add their own comments as to what's trendy.
YOUR TURN	Students work in pairs or small groups to describe their clothes, hair and accessories.
2A	Focus students' attention on the dictionary definition of 'bling'. Students discuss which of these things they wear or would like to wear. **Language note:** this neologism has entered into the language from rap and African-American culture. It is now strongly rooted in both black and white culture and has become a synonym for flashy jewellery in general. It originally referred to the sound a shop cash register makes when a sale is made "bling-ker-ching".
2B CD2 Track 29	Focus students' attention on the table. Students listen for the things Mikey and Shell wear on school days and at the weekends. Students should listen to the track twice, as happens in international examinations. **Key:** *Mikey doesn't wear jewellery at school. At the weekend he wears earrings and he sometimes wears a necklace. Shell wears earrings and a nose-ring at school. At the weekend she wears earrings and a nose-ring and bling such as a necklace and bracelet.* **Audio script** (Accents: Eng) Hi. My name's Mikey and I'm 14. I don't wear a lot of jewellery. I can't wear jewellery at school, so I don't wear anything during the week. At the weekend I wear earrings. I have one ear pierced. I wear two earrings in that ear. I sometimes wear a necklace, too. My girlfriend gave the necklace to me for my birthday. Hi. My name's Shell. I'm 15. Our school is quite relaxed about jewellery. I wear earrings during the week and at weekends. I also wear my nose-ring at school and at home. I like bling a lot, so at the weekends I wear this great necklace and bracelet. I don't like rings so I don't have any.
2C	Students discuss the jewellery they wear at the weekend.
3	**Tip:** ask whether any students are wearing wristbands and why they are wearing them. Students read these short texts about wristbands and campaigns. They match them to the cause. **Key:** 1. *B*, 2. *D*, 3. *A*, 4. *C*.
OVER TO YOU	**A** Students work together to invent a campaign, a slogan, a colour and the cost of a wristband. Prompt groups with causes such as: anti-pollution, anti-famine or anti-school, if necessary. **B** Students compare their campaigns and wristbands.
Optional Extension	Students cut out pictures of fashionable clothes from magazines and make a poster showing what's cool and trendy today.
Homework Option	Students describe the clothes they like to wear when they go out.
Web links	www.livestrong.org The website for Lance Armstrong's campaign. www.makepovertyhistory.org The anti-poverty campaign website. www.beatbullying.org The website contains lots of advice for fighting against bullies.

HISTORY AND TRADITIONS LESSON **9D**

Civil War! The English and American civil wars pp. 126-127

This lesson introduces the concept of civil wars and is designed to encourage students to approach historical sources to find out information for themselves. The culmination of the activity is the **Over to You** section where students write a history of the English Civil War, using the model given for the American Civil War.

Objectives: students will...	• learn / revise the lexis of wars • learn about the American Civil War • learn about the English Civil War • write a history of the English Civil War • understand the causes and effects of these two wars
Warm-up CD2 Track 30	Students use their general knowledge to put these events in chronological order. They then listen and check. **Key:** 1. *The English Civil War (1642-1651)*; 2. *The French Revolution (1789)*; 3. *The American Civil War (1861-1865)*; 4. *The First World War (1914-1918)*; 5. *The fall of the Berlin Wall (1989)*. **Audio script (Accent:** Eng) The English Civil War was in the seventeenth century. The French Revolution was in the eighteenth century. The American Civil War was in the nineteenth century. The First World War was at the beginning of the twentieth century. The Fall of the Berlin Wall was near the end of the twentieth century.
1A	Students should total up the civil war deaths in the table on page 127. **Key:** Total deaths in battle: *84,738* Subtotal: *100,300* Overall total: *185,038*
1B	Point out to students that they are going to play the role of history detectives. **Note:** in order to complete this exercise and answer the questions, students need to read all the information on page 126 and all the relevant information on page 127 including: the table, the texts, the timeline, the labelled pictures and the student's work. This exercise is designed to help students improve their reference skills and use skills at reading individual historical sources. **Key:** 1. *1642-1651*; 2. *King Charles I and Oliver Cromwell*; 3. *42*; 4. *The King*; 5. *Parliament*; 6. *Cromwell*; 7. *185,038 (but 84,738 were deaths in battle)*; 8. *Cromwell / Parliament*; 9. *He was executed*; 10. *Parliament got more power*.
2 CD2 Track 31	Give students a few moments to read through the text. Students listen for the information about the American Civil War. Students should listen to the track twice, as happens in international examinations. **Note:** the listening text is not identical to the one in the Student's Book as per certifications to encourage students to be less reliant on the written word and to take notes about what they hear. **Audio script and key (Accent:** USA) The American Civil War started in *1861*. It was the war between the Northern and Southern states of the USA. The Northern States wanted to abolish slavery. The Southern States wanted to keep slavery. They also wanted the states to have individual rights. The southern states were Mississippi, the Carolinas, *Florida*, Alabama, Georgia, Louisiana, *Texas*, Virginia, Arkansas and Tennessee. Their president was Jefferson Davis. The leader of the Northern States was *President* Abraham Lincoln. About 600,000 people died in the American Civil War. The *Northern States* won the war and America was united again. The Civil War ended in 1865.
OVER TO YOU	Students now have all the historical information they need and a model answer so that they can write a short history of the English Civil War.
Optional Extension	Students research another of the momentous events mentioned in the **Warm-up** activity.
Homework Option	Students work on writing a timeline for another historical event. This will help them extract the main information from a text.
Web links	www.historyplace.com/civilwar A full account of the American civil war. www.thesealedknot.org The organisation which re-enacts battles from the English Civil War. www.parliament.uk Contains information on the history of Parliament.

THE WORLD WE LIVE IN

LESSON 9E

Slaves and Prospectors
Cotton and gold in the USA — pp. 128-129

This lesson introduces two key materials which helped form modern America: cotton and gold. This involves discussion of slavery (many slaves worked on the cotton plantations in the southern states of the USA).

Objectives: students will...	• learn / revise the lexis of natural materials • learn / revise vocabulary connected with cotton and gold • learn about slaves and the slave trade • learn about the Gold Rush and gold itself • learn a typical slave song
Warm-up	Organize a class brainstorm of natural materials. The list could include: cotton, wool, silk, gold, silver, bronze, iron, wood, clay etc.
1A	Focus students' attention on the pictures and ask which pictures show cotton. **Key:** the answer is *all of them: cotton jeans, sewing cotton, a cotton T-shirt and raw cotton in the fields*.
1B	Students read the text about cotton. They then answer the True / False / Doesn't say questions. **Key:** 1. *False*, 2. *True*, 3. *Doesn't say*, 4. *True*, 5. *False*, 6. *True*.
2 CD2 Track 32	Students listen to this typical plantation song and choose the correct word. **Tip:** encourage students to sing and mime the actions to the song. The song is repeated. **Audio script and key** *Bend* down, *turn* around *Jump* down, *spin* around *Pick* a bale of cotton *Pick* a bale of cotton *Bend* down, *turn* around *Jump* down, *spin* around *Pick* a bale a day. *Pick* a bale a day.
3A 3B CD2 Track 33	The other material we are looking at in this lesson is gold. First, students try to do the gold quiz themselves. They should guess the answers if they aren't sure. Students then listen to check their answers. **Key:** 1. *A*, 2. *C*, 3. *B*, 4. *A*. **Audio script (Accent:** GB) The chemical symbol for gold is Au. Ag is silver and Al is Aluminium. The purity of gold is very important. You measure this in carats. That's C-A-R-A-T not the orange things you eat! You can find gold under ground, in mines, and in rivers. Today, the biggest reserves of gold are in South Africa, but some people say there is gold on the Moon!
4	Students complete this KET-style activity which explains one phenomenon of the Gold Rush: the boom town and the ghost town. **Key:** 1. *A*, 2. *B*, 3. *B*, 4. *C*, 5. *C*, 6. *A*.
OVER TO YOU	Students make a list of things which can be made from cotton. They then check their clothing labels and labels on their possessions to see if any of them are made of cotton.
Optional Extension	Students brainstorm things made from gold.
Homework Option	Students research another material such as silver to find out what it is, where it comes from and what it's used for.
Web links	www.yosemitegold.com The official website for Yosemite. www.ghosttowngallery.com A selection of photos relating to ghost towns left after the end of the Gold Rush. www.cottonsjourney.com The history of cotton plantations and cotton manufacturing in the USA.

64

THE CHILL ZONE 9
pp. 130-131

Spot the flag!
Key: The correct pair mirror image for the Confederate flag is *C* and for the Union flag is *B*.

SPOT THE 4 DIFFERENCES:
Key: 1. *sunglasses* (different shapes); 2. *hair* (curly and straight); 3. *wristband* (one red and one green); 4. *jeans* (one pair is stone-washed).

Swot spot
Key: 1. *False*, 2. *False*, 3. *False*, 4. *True*.

The Ka Mate Haka
CD2 Track 34 For **audio script** see Student's Book page 131.

British English or American English?
Key:

AmE	BrE
subway	underground / tube
movie theater	cinema
station wagon	estate car
zip code	post code
elevator	lift

There's gold in them there hills!
Key: *the gold is in the mountains illustrated in the second square down of the first column.*

WORKING WITH TEXTS 9
pp. 132-133

The Pilgrim Fathers and the Mayflower
This is the ninth long text in a section aimed at preparing students for state examinations. The texts are graded according to level and are progressive. Each text is followed by a series of comprehension questions and work on summary skills.

Before you read
1 Students check the meaning of these words with you or in their dictionaries.

Reading
2 Students read the text and answer the questions.
Key:
1. *Anglicanism*; 2. *Other countries, America*; 3. *Mayflower*; 4. *2 months*; 5. *At Cape Cod, New England*; 6. *New Plymouth*; 7. *Half of them*; 8. *They helped them hunt native birds*; 9. *The Pilgrims*; 10. *The Mayflower*.

Pronunciation note: Argyle /ɑːˈgaɪəl/

Summary skills
3A Students highlight the keywords and write a summary.
3B Focus students' attention on the checklist. They should be encouraged to use this type of mental checklist for all summaries they do.

65

SCHOOL LIFE AND EDUCATION **LESSON 10A**

The New York Fame School
Getting home from school in New York — pp. 134-135

This lesson looks at getting home from school in a big city as a way of introducing the sights of New York and a street map of Manhattan and the area around.

Objectives: students will...	• learn about the principal landmarks in New York • learn / revise the lexis of landmarks • learn about the NYC school for performing arts • follow a route on a map • write about their journeys home from school
Warm-up	Brainstorm the main sights of New York.
1A 1B	Students find the landmarks and the places on the map of New York City.
2A	Students read the information about Flag High school and find it on the map. **Pronunciation note:** Lincoln /ˈlɪŋkən/
2B CD2 Track 35	James Lambert is a student there. Give students a few moments to read through the student card before they listen for the missing information. Students should listen to the track twice, as happens in international examinations. **Language note:** specialty = AmE, speciality = BrE. **Key:** Age: *14*; Address: *2474 Forest Avenue*; Specialty: *Dance*; Class: *6*. **Audio script (Accent:** USA) Hi. My name's James Lambert and I'm 14 years old. I live on Staten Island and my address is 2474 (two four seven four) Forest Avenue. I love studying at Flag because I love dancing and my speciality is dance. My teacher is Emma and I'm in class 6.
2C CD2 Track 36	Students listen to the second part of the interview with James. The first time they listen, they should be listening for the answers to the comprehension questions. **Key:** 1. (Battery Park), Ellis Island, the Statue of Liberty 2. About 90 minutes / an hour and a half 3. About 15 miles **Audio script (Accent:** USA) Yeah, I have a really long trip home because I live out of Manhattan. I get the subway at 66th Street to Battery Park where I get the ferry. It's a great trip – we go past Ellis Island and the Statue of Liberty – I love that bit – it's never boring. I get off the ferry at Staten Island and walk five minutes home. My trip probably takes about 90 minutes. It's not very far, but it takes an hour and a half, yeah, an hour and a half. It's about 15 miles.
2D CD2 Track 37	Students listen to the interview a second time. This time they follow James' route on the map of New York.
OVER TO YOU	Students write a short letter to James talking about their trip home. **Note:** this is a KET-style writing activity.
Optional Extension	Students research a New York landmark such as the Statue of Liberty. This could be an Internet project or they could find the information from an encyclopaedia.
Homework Option	Students think about the advantages and disadvantages of being famous.
Web links	www.laguardiahs.org The high school website. www.mta.info Information about public transport in New York. www.siferry.com The timetable and photos of the New York ferries.

PEOPLE AND LIFESTYLES

LESSON 10B

Culture within a Culture
The Amish and Native Americans
pp. 136-137

This lesson addresses two different groups and cultures to be found in the USA: the Amish and Native Americans.
Pronunciation note: Amish /ˈɑːmɪʃ/

Objectives: students will...	• learn / revise the lexis of modern gadgets • learn about Amish and Cherokee culture • learn about the true story of Pocahontas • compare their lives with Amish lives • learn about animal tracking
Warm-up	Brainstorm what students know about the Amish and Native Americans.
1A	Before students read the text, point out the photos and elicit things which seem unusual to them.
1B	Students read the FAQs from a website and match them with the answers. **Pronunciation note:** students should know that the individual letters in FAQs are sounded. F.A.Qs /ef//eɪ//kjuːz/ **Key:** a) *3*, b) *5*, c) *6*, d) *2*, e) *4*, f) *1*.
YOUR TURN	Students look at the modern day household gadgets and equipment and decide which they would find difficult to live without and why.
2 **CD2 Track 38**	The next group we look at is one tribe of American Indians, the Cherokee. Students read the information in the text before they listen and then listen to find the missing information. Students should listen twice as happens in international examinations. **Audio script and key (Accent:** USA**)** The Cherokee is a Native American tribe. Many people say their name means 'fire'. They are traditionally from *Oklahoma*. There are *seven* different Cherokee clans. They have seven different directions, not four: they are North, South, East, West but also Up, *Down* and *Centre*. Centre is where you are. The Cherokee have four sacred colours: *red, blue, black* and *white*. The Cherokee never lived in tepees. Their houses were made of mud or wood. Today they live in normal houses, except some who live in traditional wooden houses. One of the traditional Cherokee foods was *popcorn*. The men had tattoos. The traditional *musical instruments* were drums, flutes and trumpets. Today there are 260,000 Cherokee. About 90,000 live in the Cherokee Nation.
OVER TO YOU	Students learn that one of the major skills developed by Native Americans was that of tracking animals. They match the tracks to the animals. **Key:** A. *Bear*; B. *Mouse*; C. *Wolf*; D. *Deer*; E. *Wild turkey*; F. *Bobcat*.
EXPLODE THE MYTH!!	**Pronunciation note:** Powhatan /ˈpaʊətæn/
Optional Extension	Students research another American Indian tribe such as the Apache.
Homework Option	Students write about the modern item they would find it most difficult to live without and explain why.
Web links	www.powhatan.org The official website of the Powhatan Renape Nation (an Amerindian reservation in New Jersey). www.nativetech.org The Native American technology and art website. www.religioustolerance.org/amish.htm Information about the Amish.

SPORT & LEISURE

LESSON 10C

Music — From bebop to hip hop

pp. 138-139

This lesson introduces the topic of popular music and the history of pop.
Pronunciation note: bebop /ˈbiːbɒp/

Objectives: students will...	• learn / revise the lexis of musical instruments • learn the names of some different genres of music • learn about decades related to music • compare their favourite types of music • read an interview with a pop group
Warm-up	Ask students to talk about their favourite singers and bands and the different types of music they like. **Tip:** you might like to ask students whether they play any musical instruments. Also, classical music is not dealt with in this unit so this would be a good point to discuss that.
1A CD2 Track 39 **1B** CD2 Track 40	Students do a music quiz. It is designed so that students can complete the whole quiz and then listen to check their answers, so there are two distinct audio scripts: one with the questions and one with the answers. **1A Audio script with questions** (Accents: GB) How much do you now about music? Try this music quiz! Question 1. Listen and match the sound to the photo. Students hear these sounds: bass guitar, synthesiser, electric guitar, drums. Question 2. Match the picture to the type of music. Focus students' attention on the photos in the book. Question 3. Listen and match the decade to the music. Students hear punk, Beatles, hip hop, disco music. Question 4. Match the photo to the decades above. Focus students' attention on the photos in the book. **1B Audio script with oral key** (Accents: GB) Question 1 Number 1. This sound is the bass guitar. [+ sound] Number 2. This sound is the synthesiser. [+ sound] Number 3. This sound is the electric guitar. [+ sound] Number 4. This sound is the drums. [+ sound] Question 2 Picture A shows a punk. Picture B shows a reggae artist. Picture C Elvis Presley. He was the King of Rock n Roll. Picture D shows a rap artist. Question 3 Number 1. This is music from the 1980s. [music] Number 2. This is music from the 1960s. [music] Number 3. This is music from the 1990s. [music] Number 4. This is music from the 1970s. [music] Question 4 Photo 1 is from the 1980s. Photo 2 is from the 1990s. Photo 3 is from the 1970s. Photo 4 is from the 1960s.
YOUR TURN	Students decide which decade is the best for music.
2A 2B CD2 Track 41	This is an interview with a new girl band from a teen magazine. Students write the questions needed to elicit these responses. They then listen and check. There may be slight variations in the questions. **Audio script and key** (Accents: Fran = GB, Bianca = Eng.) FRAN *How did you meet?* BIANCA We met at school. We played our first gig at school for a school disco. It was great! FRAN *What was the name of your first song?* BIANCA "Buzzin" was the name of our first song. It was also our first hit! FRAN *What's it about?* BIANCA It's about being good friends and feeling good. FRAN *When are you going on tour?* BIANCA We're going on tour in September. Our first big gig is in Manchester. We're all really excited about it. FRAN *What's your favourite colour?* BIANCA My favourite colour is yellow, but I like pink as well – but not together. FRAN *Who's your favourite band?* BIANCA It may sound old fashioned but my favourite band is actually the Beatles. I just think they're blazin'.
3	Students discuss what songs, luxuries and books they would take with them if they had to live on a desert island. Students compare their choices with a partner.
OVER TO YOU	This is a KET-style speaking activity. Student A reads the information about the rock concert. Student B asks questions using the prompts. They should then swap roles.
Optional Extension	Students write an interview for their favourite pop singer or group.
Homework Option	Students write about their favourite pop group or pop singer.
Web links	www.museum.tv The Museum of Broadcast Communications in the USA. www.oldiesmusic.com History, trivia and charts related to 50s-70s music. www.mtv.com The MTV home page.

HISTORY AND TRADITIONS

LESSON 10D

"We the people..." Constitutions and political systems

pp. 140-141

This lesson addresses the issue of the US constitution and the political system in the UK and the USA.
Culture note: "We the people.." is the opening line of the constitution of the United States of America.

Objectives: students will...	• learn / revise the lexis of government • understand about the political system in the USA and UK • learn about the American Constitution • discuss rights and obligations
Warm-up	Ask students whether they are interested in politics and why / why not.
1A	Students read the information about the political division of the UK and draw lines on the map to focus on the geographical location of the four divisions. **Pronunciation note:** Edinburgh /ˈedɪnbrə/
1B	Students answer the True / False / Doesn't say questions about political power in the UK. **Key:** 1. *True*, 2. *False*, 3. *Doesn't say*, 4. *False*.
2	This exercise shifts the focus to the USA. Students read the article and complete the diagram. **Key:** | EXECUTIVE	LEGISLATIVE	JUDICIAL
---	---	---
The president	Congress	The Supreme Court
The Cabinet	Senate	The House of Representatives	
3 CD2 Track 42	Give students a few moments to read through the text. Students listen for the missing information. Students should listen to the track twice, as happens in international examinations. **Audio script and key (Accent:** USA) George Washington was one of the framers of the Constitution. He was born in *1732*. He didn't go to *school*, he studied at home. He was a farmer and then became a soldier. He was the commander of the army during the American Revolution. He later became the *first* President of the United States of America. He was a very tall man. His favourite food was *ice-cream*. He liked fishing and *horse-riding*. He had very strange false teeth – they were made of gold, ivory and *horse* and donkey teeth! George Washington designed the capital city of America, Washington DC. His picture is on the American one-dollar bill. He died in *1799*.
YOUR TURN	Students can surf the net to find out about a famous statesman or woman from their country.
OVER TO YOU	**A** Focus students' attention on the Bill of Rights and the amendments to the American Constitution. Ask students which were added in 1787 and which came later. This is to focus on the point in time when some of today's rights were achieved. **Key:** 1. *A*, 2. *C*, 3. *D*, 4. *B*. **B** Students work together to think about a constitution for their school.
Optional Extension	Students write about the political system in their country.
Homework Option	Students write a biography of a politician past or present.
Web links	www.usconstitution.net Lots of activities related to the US Constitution. www.congressforkids.net Information about the political system in the USA. www.wales.gov.uk Information about the Welsh Assembly.

THE WORLD WE LIVE IN

LESSON 10E

Inventors and Inventions
Famous English-speaking inventors pp. 142-143

This lesson introduces famous inventors and inventions from the ESW.

Objectives: students will...	• learn about inventions • match inventions to years • re-order a text • discuss the most important inventions in history • present their own invention to the class
Warm-up	Elicit from students how much they know about the invention of the telephone.
1A	Point out to students that different countries dispute who actually invented the phone. Students read about these different inventors. The purpose of this activity is for students to read the information and then make up their own minds as to whose invention it was.
1B	Students give their opinions using the template: *I think x invented the phone because xxx*.
2A 2B CD2 Track 43	Students now try and guess what year these inventions came from. Play the track so that students can listen and check. **Key:** 1. *1928*; 2. *1972*; 3. *1904*; 4. *2004*; 5. *1921*; 6. *1974*. **Audio script** (**Accent:** GB) The earliest of these inventions is the teabag. It was invented in 1904. Next comes the lie-detector. It was invented in 1921. Honestly! Then comes bubble gum. People started blowing bubbles in 1928. Next we jump to the seventies with the first videogame. That was a game called Pong invented in 1972. Also in the seventies, we have post-it notes. They were invented in 1974. Finally, in 2004, we have the invention of the thinking shoes. They have a microchip.
YOUR TURN	Students decide which they think is the most important invention.
3A 3B CD2 Track 44	This activity goes into more detail about the invention of post-it notes. Students put the extracts into the correct order. They then listen to check their order. **Audio script and key** (**Accent:** USA) Spence Silver was a chemist. One day, he was playing with different types of glue mixes. He found a glue that was really useless. It didn't dry and it wasn't very sticky! He had one idea. He covered a notice board with the glue. People could put papers on it then take them off again. Nobody really needed it. A second chemist called Arthur Fry knew about this glue. He was the director of a choir. He needed a temporary way to mark the pages in his choir book. The post-it was born!
4	Students look at the inventions in the photos and decide which is the most important. Encourage students to justify their choices.
OVER TO YOU	**A** Students work in pairs to invent a new pen, car, entertainments system or phone. If time allows, students can produce a leaflet to illustrate their new invention and to help them present their idea to the class. **B** Students present their ideas to the class. Display the leaflets on the wall.
Optional Extension	Use exercise 4 as a balloon debate activity, where students vote as a group to discard inventions.
Homework Option	Students research the history of another invention, such as the videogame console.
Web links	www.telephonetribute.com A website full of information about the telephone. www.wanderlist.com/inventions Students can vote for what they think is the most important invention ever in the history of the world. www.enchantedlearning.com/inventors An American kids' site with an A-Z of inventions and inventors.

THE CHILL ZONE 10

pp. 144-145

Song: "Fame"

CD2 Track 45 Audio script and key:

Baby look at me
And tell me what you *see*
You ain't seen the best of me yet
Give me time, I'll make you forget the rest.
I got a story, and you can set it free
I can catch the moon in my hand
Don't you *know* who I am?

Chorus:
Remember my name (Fame)
I'm gonna *live* forever
I'm gonna learn how to fly (High)
I feel it coming together
People will see me and die (Fame)
I'm gonna make it to heaven
Light up the sky like a flame (Fame)
I'm gonna *live* forever
Baby, *remember* my name
Remember, Remember, Remember, Remember,
Remember, Remember, Remember, Remember

Baby hold me tight
And you can make it right.
You can shoot me straight to the top
Give me *love* and take all I've got to give.
Baby I'm in love
Too much is not enough
I surround your heart to embrace
You *know* I got what it takes.

Repeat Chorus

Swot spot
Key: 1. a, 2. a, 3. c, 4. c.

Code crackers
Key: 1. *Navajo*, 2. *Arizona*.

WORKING WITH TEXTS 10

pp. 146-147

The Industrial Revolution

This is the final long text in a section aimed at preparing students for state examinations. The texts are graded according to level and are progressive. Each text is followed by a series of comprehension questions and work on summary skills.

Before you read
1 Students complete the table by adding 2 more things to each list.

Reading
2 Students read the text and answer the questions.
Key: 1. *The Industrial Revolution*; 2. *Agricultural*; 3. *Newcomen*; 4. *Handloom weavers from the Midlands, they smashed the new machines*; 5. *Canals, roads, the railway*; 6. *Huskisson was killed by the train*; 7. *It went from less than 10,000 to 800,000*; 8. *To stop child labour*; 9. *A building made from glass and iron.*

Pronunciation note: Luddites /ˈlʌdaɪts/

Summary skills
3A Students write a title for each paragraph. This could be in the form of a question or a statement.

3B Students now write a summary of the text. **Tip:** point out the checklist area in the **Top Tip!** box.

71

ESW Profiles

This entire section is conceived as an interactive encyclopaedic file on the principal nations which make up the English-speaking world. The main information about each place such as the capital, languages, currency, holidays and Internet code are all given so that students can use these pages as a reference when necessary. In addition, each country's profile looks in more detail at one aspect of the country concerned. These **Focus on** sections are as follows:

	FOCUS ON
Australia and New Zealand	Zoology
Canada	Geography
The Commonwealth	Cooperation
India	Endangered species
Ireland	Archaeology
The United Kingdom	Meteorology
The United States	Geology

PROFILE ON... Australia and New Zealand   pp. 148-149

1A Focus students' attention on the map. They should be able to extrapolate the capitals and five other important cities from Australia and three from New Zealand.
Key: Australia: Capital = *Canberra*; five other important cities are: *Perth, Adelaide, Melbourne, Sydney, Brisbane*.
New Zealand: Capital = *Wellington*; other important cities are: *Auckland, Christchurch and Dunedin*.
Pronunciation note: Dunedin /dʌˈniːdɪn/

1B Students extract the information on national emblems from the table.
Key: Australia: *kangaroo & emu*; New Zealand: *kiwi*.

2A Students look at the quiz and try to guess the answers.
Key: 1. *A*, 2. *C*, 3. *B*, 4. *A*.

2B CD2 Track 46
Students listen to check.
Audio script and key (**Accents:** Q. = GB, A. = USA.)
(Q.) 1. What's the population of Australia? (A.) *20 million* people live in Australia.
(Q.) 2. What's the population of New Zealand? (A.) New Zealand has a small population, just *4 million*.
(Q.) 3. What are the indigenous peoples of Australia and New Zealand called? (A.) The indigenous people of Australia are called the *Aboriginals*. In New Zealand they are called the *Maori*.
(Q.) 4. What's the highest Mountain in New Zealand? (A.) The highest mountain in New Zealand is called *Mount Cook*.

3 Students read the description of the flag and label the two.
Key: A = *Australian flag*; B = *New Zealand flag*.

Focus on... Zoology

4A Students read the descriptions and match them to the coins.
Key: 1. *B*, 2. *F*, 3. *A*, 4. *G*, 5. *C*, 6. *D*, 7. *E*.

4B Take a handful of coins from your country into class. Ask students if there are any pictures of animals on them.

4C This is possible to set as a research homework. Students write about a wild animal which is native to their country.

Pronunciation note:

kotuku	/ˈkɔːtʊkʊ/
platypus	/ˈplætɪpəs/
echidna	/ɪˈkɪdnə/
lyrebird	/ˈlaɪəbɜːd/
tuatara	/ˌtuːəˈtɑːrə/

Web links   www.australia.com   www.australia.gov.au   www.govt.nz   www.mch.govt.nz

PROFILE ON... Canada   pp. 150-151

1A	Focus students' attention on the map. They should be able to extrapolate the capital and five other important cities from Canada. They should also look at the borders. **Key:** Capital = *Ottawa*; five other important cities are: *Montreal, Toronto, Québec, Vancouver and Calgary*; Canada shares a border with *the USA*.
1B	Students extract the information on national emblems from the table. **Key:** *maple leaf* and *American beaver*.
2A	Students look at the quiz and try to guess the answers. **Key:** 1. *B*, 2. *A*, 3. *C*, 4. *A*.
2B CD2 Track 47	Students listen to check. **Audio script and key** (**Accents:** Q. = Eng, A. = Can.) (Q.) 1. What's the population of Canada? (A.) *32 million* people live in Canada. (Q.) 2. What's the area of Canada? (A.) The area of Canada is about *10 million square kilometres*. (Q.) 3. What percentage of people speak English? (A.) About *60%* of the population speak English. (Q.) 4. What is Canada's second language? (A.) Canada's second language is *French*.
3	Students read the short text and answer the comprehension questions. **Key:** 1. *Maple leaf*; 2. *C*; 3. *Yes*; 4. *Queen Elizabeth II*; 5. *Deer, bear, duck*.
Focus on... **Geography**	Students read the text and study the pictures. **Key:** **4A** Canada: Population density = *3* people per km^2; coastline = *243,791 km*; *Toronto* is the largest city with a population of *2.4 million* people; Mount *Logan* is *5,959* metres high; the River Mackenzie is *1,640* km long; the lowest ever temperature in the Yukon was *-63°C*. **4B** Students complete the table about their own country. **4C** This is possible to set as a writing homework. Students write about their own country's geography using the information in the text as a model.
Web links	www.gc.ca www.canada.travel

PROFILE ON... The Commonwealth   pp. 152-153

1	Focus students' attention on the map. They should be able to extrapolate the headquarters of the Commonwealth and the largest country in terms of area. **Key:** Headquarters = *London*; Largest country by area = *Canada*.
2A	Students look at the quiz and try to guess the answers. **Key:** 1. *B*, 2. *A*, 3. *A*, 4. *C*.
2B CD2 Track 48	Students listen to check. **Audio script and key** (**Accents:** Q. = GB, A. = Eng.) (Q.) 1. What's the official language of the Commonwealth? (A.) There's only one official language of the Commonwealth – that's *British English*. (Q.) 2. Which Commonwealth country has the largest population? (A.) *India* is the country with the largest population. It's enormous, more than a billion people. (Q.) 3. When was the Commonwealth founded? (A.) The modern Commonwealth was founded in *1949*. (Q.) 4. On what continents can you find members of the Commonwealth? (A.) On *six continents*: Africa, Australia & Oceania, Europe, North & South America, Asia and Antarctica.
3A	Students match the flags to the descriptions. **Key:** 1. *C*, 2. *E*, 3. *A*, 4. *B*, 5. *D*.
3B	Students decide which continents the countries belong to. **Key:** Africa: *Ghana*; Asia: *Singapore*; Australia and Oceania: *The Solomon Islands*; Europe: *Malta*; The Americas: *Jamaica*.
Focus on... **Cooperation**	**4A** Students read the text and complete the table. **Key:** | The number of member countries is	53
The number of people in those countries is	1.7 billion
The Commonwealth was founded in	1949
The country with the largest population is	India
The country with the smallest population is	Tuvalu
The Commonwealth Games are held every	4 years | **4B** Students tick the international organizations their country belongs to.
Web links	www.thecommonwealth.org www.cia.gov/cia/publications/factbook

PROFILE ON... India
pp. 154-155

1A	Focus students' attention on the map. They should be able to extrapolate the capital and five other important cities from the map. **Key:** Capital = *New Delhi*; five other important cities are: *Mumbai* (ex Bombay), *Delhi*, *Bangalore*, *Kolkata* (ex Calcutta), *Chennai* (ex Madras).
1B	Students extract the information on the national emblem from the table. **Key:** *The Ashoka Capital*
2A	Students look at the quiz and try to guess the answers. **Key:** 1. *B*, 2. *A*, 3. *C*, 4. *B*.
2B CD2 Track 49	Students listen to check. **Audio script and key** (**Accents:** Q. = Eng, A. = Ind.) (Q.) 1. What's the population of India? (A.) There are just over *1.1 billion* people who live in India. It's the second largest population in the world. (Q.) 2. How many official languages are there in India? (A.) There are actually *twenty-three* official languages in India. They include Hindi and English. (Q.) 3. The highest mountain in India is Kangchenjunga. How high is it? (A.) The highest mountain is in the Himalayas on the border with Nepal. It's *8,586 m* high. (Q.) 4. What type of state is India? (A.) India is a *republic*. It became a *republic* in 1947.
3	Students read the text, look at the photos of the 10 rupee note and answer the questions. **Key:** 1. *Mahatma Gandhi*; 2. *17 (English, Hindi and 15 others)*; 3. *Rhino, tiger and elephant*.
Focus on... Endangered species	**4A** Students read the descriptions and complete the table **Key:** |	Bengal tiger	Indian elephant	Indian Rhinoceros
---	---	---	---
Length	3 m	about 6.5 m	3.5 m
Height	about 1 m	4 m	1.8 m
Weight	220 kg	5 tonnes	3 tonnes
Diet	carnivore	herbivore	herbivore
Habitat	forests	varied	forests and grasslands
Population	4,600	30,000	2,300
In danger from (reason)	man (for skins and medicines)	man (for ivory tusks and because they damage crops)	man (the horn is used in traditional medicine)	 **4B** This exercise could be done as homework: students write about the Indian rhinoceros using the information in the table.
Web links	www.india.gov.in www.tourismindia.com

PROFILE ON... Ireland
pp. 156-157

1A	Focus students' attention on the map. They should be able to extrapolate the capital and five other important cities from Ireland. **Key:** Capital = *Dublin*; five other important cities are: *Cork, Waterford, Galway, Dundalk, Limerick*.
1B	Students extract the information on national emblems from the table. **Key:** *harp* and *shamrock*
2A	Students look at the quiz and try to guess the answers. **Key:** 1. *A*, 2. *A*, 3. *B*, 4. *B*.
2B CD2 Track 50	Students listen to check. **Audio script and key** (**Accents:** Q. = Eng, A. = Irish.) (Q.) 1. What's the population of Ireland? (A.) The population of Ireland is about *4.1 million*. (Q.) 2. What are the two official languages of Ireland? (A.) The two official languages are *English and Irish*. (Q.) 3. The longest river is the Shannon. How long is it? (A.) It's *386 km* long. (Q.) 4. What was the highest temperature ever recorded? (A.) It isn't usually very, very hot in Ireland, but in 1887 the highest temperature was recorded. This was *33.3° C*.
3	Students read the short introduction and match the descriptions to the coins. **Key:** 1. *B*, 2. *C*, 3. *D*, 4. *A*.
Focus on... Archaeology	**4A** Students read the text and answer the questions: **Key:** 1. *Boyne Valley*. 2. *More than 5,200 years old*. 3. *The sun lights up the long passage* 4. *About 200,000*. **4B** Students write about or discuss the most famous archaeological sites in their countries.
Web links	www.irlgov.ie www.tourismireland.com

PROFILE ON... The UK

pp. 158-159

1A	Focus students' attention on the map. They should be able to extrapolate the capitals and five other important cities from the UK. **Key:** Capital = *London*; Regional capitals = *Belfast, Edinburgh* and *Cardiff*; five other important cities are: *Birmingham, Manchester, Glasgow, Leeds, Liverpool.* **Pronunciation note:** Edinburgh /ˈɛdɪnbrə/
1B	Students extract the information on national emblems of Scotland and Wales. **Key:** *Thistle* (Scotland) and *dragon* (Wales)
2A	Students look at the quiz and try to guess the answers. **Key:** 1. *A*, 2. *C*, 3. *A*, 4. *B*.
2B CD2 Track 51	Students listen to check. **Audio script and key** (**Accents**: Q. = Eng, A. = Eng.) (Q.) 1. What's the population of the UK? (A.) The population of the UK is just under *60 million.* (Q.) 2. What's the population of Scotland? (A.) Well, about 50 million people live in England, about 3 million live in Wales, about 1 million 750 thousand people live in Northern Ireland and about *5 million* people live in Scotland. (Q.) 3. How many official languages are there in the UK? (A.) There are actually *six languages* used officially in the UK: English, Welsh, Scottish Gaelic, Cornish, Irish, Scots. (Q.) 4. The highest mountain in the UK is Ben Nevis. How high is it? (A.) Ben Nevis is in Scotland. It isn't very high. In fact, it's only *1,344 m* high.
3	Students read the short introduction and match the descriptions to the coins **Key**: 1. *B*, 2. *E*, 3. *D*, 4. *A*, 5. *C*.
Focus on... Meteorology	**4A** Students read the text and answer the questions. **Key:** 1. *Tropical air from the south meets cold polar air from the north*; 2. *Autumn*; 3. *The Lake District*; 4. *The South East of England*. **4B** Students write a paragraph about the weather in their countries.
Web links	www.direct.gov.uk www.royal.gov.uk www.visitbritain.com

PROFILE ON... The USA

pp. 160-161

1A	Focus students' attention on the map. They should be able to extrapolate the capital and two countries which border the USA. **Key:** Capital = *Washington DC*; bordering countries are *Mexico* and *Canada*.
1B	Students mark the five largest cities on the map. **Key:** From left to right these are *Los Angeles, Houston, Chicago, Philadelphia, New York*.
1C	Students extract the information on the national emblem from the table. **Key:** *the bald eagle*.
2A	Students look at the quiz and try to guess the answers. **Key:** 1. *B*, 2. *A*, 3. *A*, 4. *B*.
2B CD2 Track 52	Students listen to check. **Audio script and key** (**Accents:** Q. = GB, A. = USA.) (Q.) 1. What's the population of The USA? (A.) The population of the USA is *300 million* at the moment. (Q.) 2. How many states are there? (A.) There are now *50* states in the USA. The last state to join was Hawaii in 1959. (Q.) 3. When is American Independence Day? (A.) It is celebrated on *July 4th*. (Q.) 4. What's the largest city in the USA? (A.) That's *New York*. It has about 8 million inhabitants.
3	Students match the questions and answers. **Key:** 1. *D*, 2. *A*, 3. *B*, 4. *C*.
Focus on... Geology	**4A** Students read the text and answer the questions True, False or Doesn't say. **Key:** 1. *False*; 2. *False*; 3. *Doesn't say*; 4. *True*; 5 *False*. **4B** Students discuss any active volcanoes there may be in their countries. This could be homework research.
Web links	www.firstgov.gov www.cia.gov/cia/publications/factbook

Lesson **2E** – **Extreme Weather** (pp. 30 – 31)

Worksheet

Part one. Observe the weather every day for a week. Write the date and record your information in the table below. Don't forget to include information about wind direction and rainfall.

Date	Temperature	Weather conditions	Other info
Monday _____	Highest: _____ Lowest: _____		
Tuesday _____	Highest: _____ Lowest: _____		
Wednesday _____	Highest: _____ Lowest: _____		
Thursday _____	Highest: _____ Lowest: _____		
Friday _____	Highest: _____ Lowest: _____		
Saturday _____	Highest: _____ Lowest: _____		

Part two. Complete the table.

The highest temperature this week was:	degrees Centigrade.
The lowest temperature this week was:	degrees Centigrade.
The average temperature this week was:	degrees Centigrade.
The highest rainfall this week was:	centimetres.
The lowest rainfall this week was:	centimetres.
The average rainfall this week was:	centimetres.

Crossing Cultures © ELI   Photocopiable

Lesson 5E – Evolution (pp. 72-73)

Photocopiable   Crossing Cultures © ELI

Lesson 7D – The Age of Discovery (pp. 98-99)

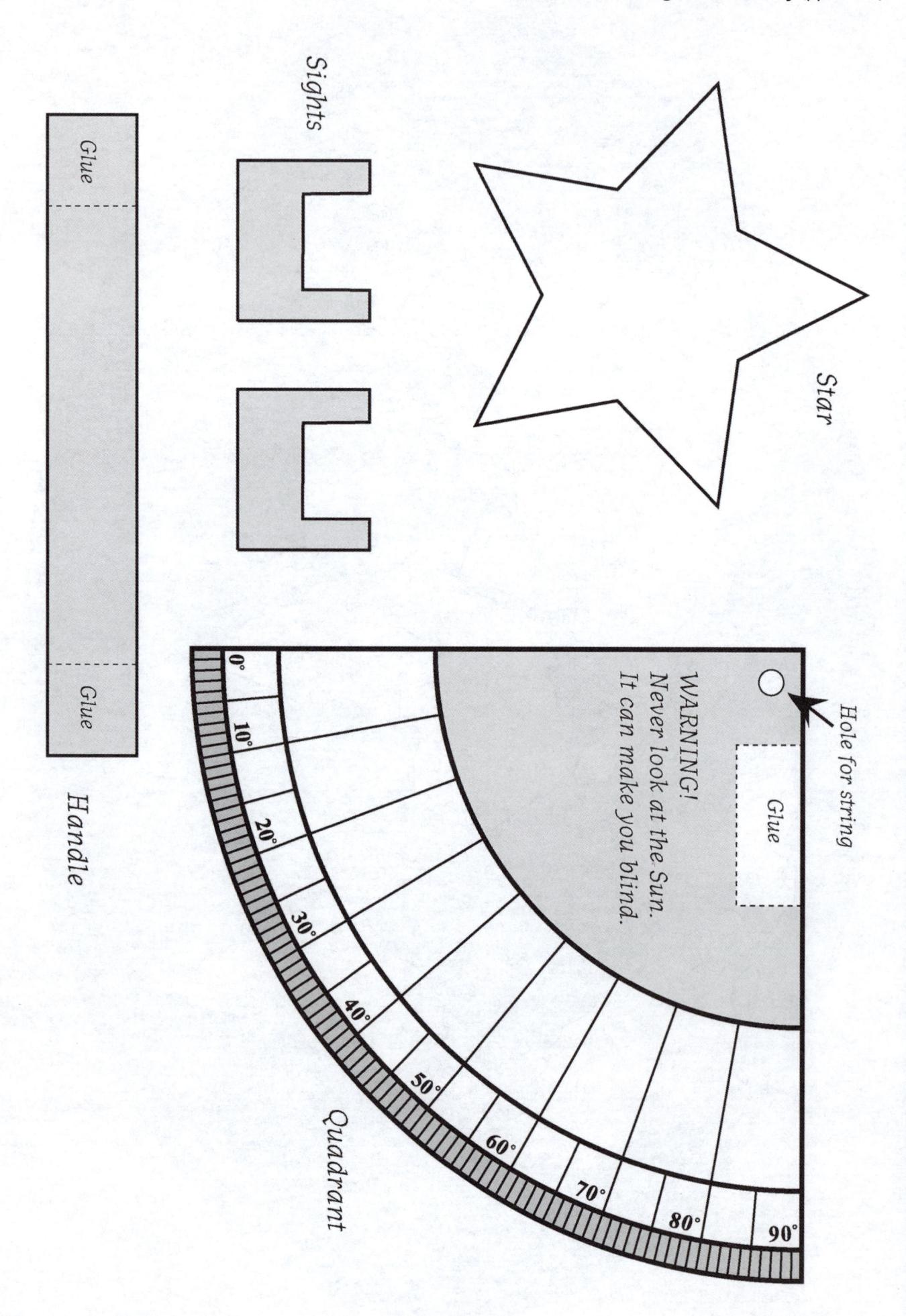

Sights

Star

Glue

Glue

Handle

0°
10°
20°
30°
40°
50°
60°
70°
80°
90°

Quadrant

WARNING!
Never look at the Sun.
It can make you blind.

Glue

Hole for string

Crossing Cultures © ELI

Photocopiable

Lesson 8A – Home Education (pp. 106 – 107)

Worksheet

Part one – pH
Use the Universal Indicator paper provided by your teacher and test the household products. Colour in the area of the table with the colour the paper goes.

Product	Colour	pH	My product is ...
I tested _____			Acid _____ Alkaline _____ Neutral _____
I tested _____			Acid _____ Alkaline _____ Neutral _____
I tested _____			Acid _____ Alkaline _____ Neutral _____
I tested _____			Acid _____ Alkaline _____ Neutral _____
I tested _____			Acid _____ Alkaline _____ Neutral _____

Part two – Hazard warnings
OVER TO YOU (p. 107). Draw your hazard warning symbols in the spaces below.

Hazard	Hazard	Hazard	My own hazard warning idea
Too much homework	A test tomorrow	An angry teacher	_____
My symbol	**My symbol**	**My symbol**	**My symbol**

Photocopiable   Crossing Cultures © ELI

Reference and key to ESW Map (CD-Rom 2)

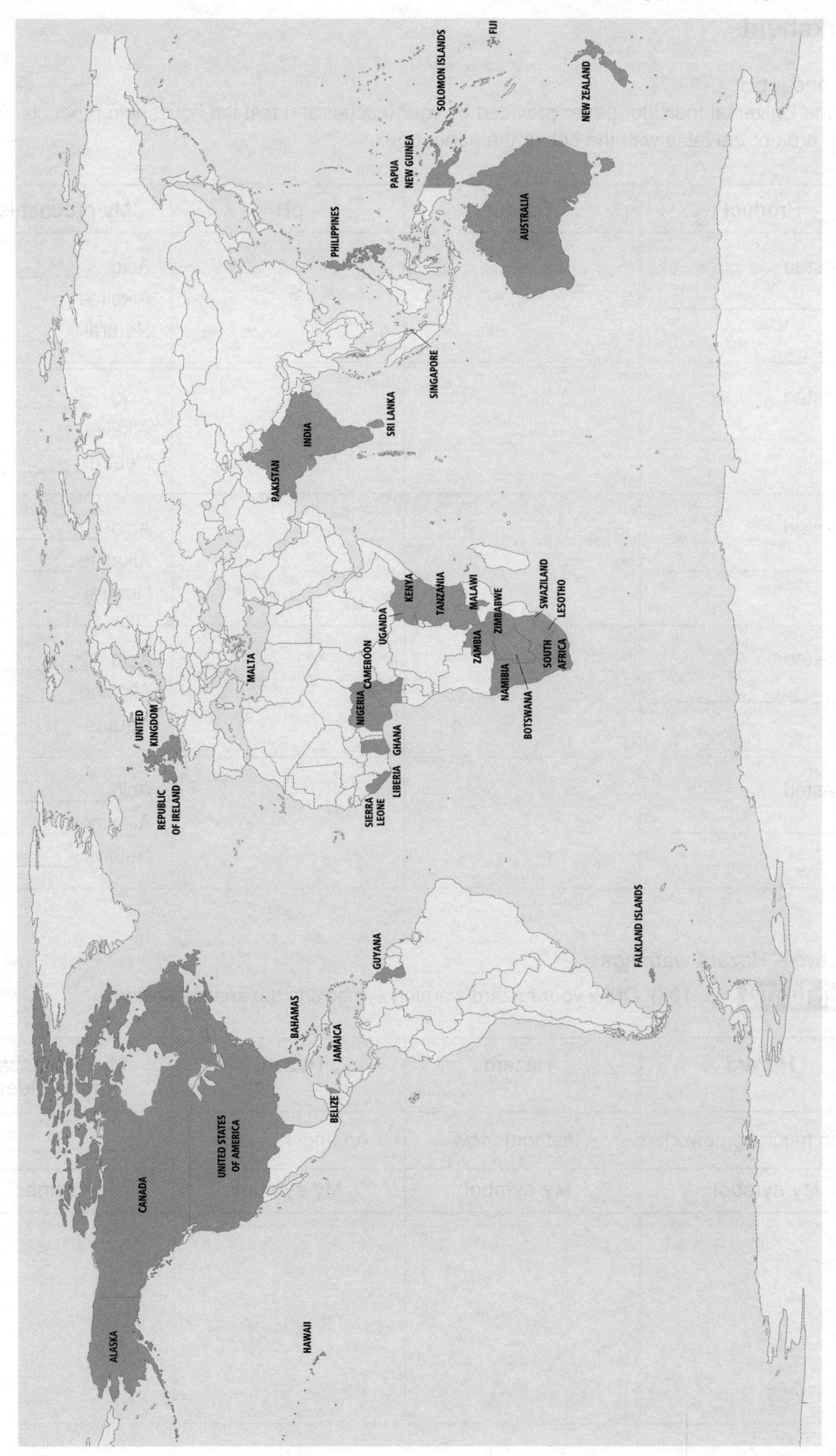

TESTS

Introduction

On the following pages you will find a test for each lesson in Crossing Cultures.

The tests are divided into blocks, with a page per block. You can photocopy these pages and cut and paste them to suit your needs. You can therefore choose to use these tests in a variety of ways, for example, after completing each lesson, after completing each block or after completing each cross-curricular pathway.

You will find that each test is either testing the general knowledge acquired from studying the lesson, or it is testing the language skills acquired from studying the lesson. Tests vary in type. There are true / false-style questions, straightforward questions requiring an answer, tests where students need to fill the blanks and tests where students choose the correct alternative. There are also more open-ended tests where students are required to write a description, a list, a letter or give their opinions and reasons for those opinions.

Name _____   Date: _____ Class _____

TEST - Block 1

1A
1. Write the correct preposition:
   a) _____ car. b) _____ foot.
2. Name 8 forms of transport.
   ....
3. Name 4 countries that use the mile.
   ....
4. How many km are there in a mile? ....

1B Write the correct verb.

1. _____ the car
2. _____ the fish
3. _____ the bathroom
4. _____ the table
5. _____ the grass
6. _____ the bed
7. _____ the ironing
8. _____ the rubbish

1C
1. Write the name of the scout badge you get for the following activities.

   a. Recognize Orion in winter, Leo in spring, Cygnus in summer and Pegasus in autumn.
   b. Have a conversation in a foreign language for about ten minutes.
   c. Keep a record of weather conditions for at least two weeks.
   d. Cook a balanced meal for 4 – 6 people.
   e. Paint or draw a landscape.
   f. Capsize in a river.
   g. Take part in 4 different climbs.
   h. Write, plan and act a play or sketch.

2. Which of the following is <u>not</u> part of the circus skills badge? Circle the correct answer.

   a. juggling
   b. trapeze
   c. handstands
   d. map-reading
   e. trick-cycling
   f. clowning

1D Complete the text about Halloween.

People celebrate Halloween in the UK and **1.**_____ , the USA and the other English-speaking nations on 31st **2.**_____. Children dress up as ghosts, goblins, witches, wizards, skeletons and, of course, Harry Potter! They make pumpkin lanterns called Jack o'Lanterns, with a **3.**_____ inside. Why do they do this? In ancient times, the **4.**_____ had a festival called Samhain at the beginning of **5.**_____. It was also the festival of the dead…. that's spooky! The Celtic tradition is still alive today, but we call it Halloween.

Today, children in the UK have Halloween parties and play games. In America, children visit the **6.**_____ in their area and knock on doors. They say "**7.**_____ or treat?" If they get a treat, it's usually **8.**_____ or chocolate. If they get nothing, they play a trick.

1E a) Where do the following animals come from?

ANIMAL	COUNTRY	ADJECTIVE
Koala		
Skunk		
Katipo		
Giant galliwasp		
Bobcat		
Kiwi		
Cobra		

b) Write an adjective to describe each animal.

Name _____   Date: _____   Class _____

TEST – Block 2

2A Answer the questions.

1. What do the letters P.E. stand for?
2. Which sport is played on grass in the UK but on ice in the USA?
3. Name six sports that use a ball.
4. Name three sports where you hit a ball.
5. Name three sports where you throw a ball.

2B Write a paragraph about your favourite food and drink.

2C Write a list of ten different types of television programme.

1. .... 6. ....
2. .... 7. ....
3. .... 8. ....
4. .... 9. ....
5. .... 10. ....

2D Answer the questions.

1. What happens if you break a mirror?
2. What happens if you hang a horseshoe in the shape of an "n"?
3. How many leaves has a lucky clover got?
4. What should you do if you see one magpie?
5. Is it lucky to see a black cat in Britain and Ireland?
6. When do people in the USA say it's lucky to eat black-eyed peas?

2E Fill the blanks in the text.

Lots of disasters are caused every year by **1.**_____ (also called cyclones or typhoons) and **2.**_____ (also called twisters). Hurricanes are circles of **3.**_____. They can be 300 km across. They bring rain and strong **4.**_____. In the Northern hemisphere a hurricane moves **5.**_____, in the Southern hemisphere it moves **6.**_____. In the centre of a hurricane – the eye – it is very calm.
We measure hurricanes in numbers: category **7.**_____ is the weakest, category **8.**_____ is the strongest. Winds in a hurricane can reach 120 km/h.
In **9.**_____ 2005 hurricane Katrina hit **10.**_____ _____, USA. The hurricane killed 1,420 people. It made many thousands of people homeless. Names are given to hurricanes. They are boys and girls' names in alphabetical order. They start again from A every year.

Photocopiable   Crossing Cultures © ELI

Name _____   Date: _____ Class _____

TEST - Block 3

3A 1. Write five activities you can do at a summer camp in the USA.
....
....

2. Complete this email.

Dear everyone,
I'm having a fantastic time at camp in America. Everyday we ....
....
I like ……………………………….. but I don't like ………………………………….
See you next month. Love ……………………………….

3B **Describe your bedroom.**
....
....

3C 1. Name two things that you can buy in each of the following places.

a. Clothes shop _____ _____   **c.** Café _____ _____   **e.** Supermarket _____ _____
b. Electrical shop _____ _____   **d.** Shoe shop _____ _____

2. Name 3 tips for shopping in the UK.

Tip 1: ....
Tip 2: ....
Tip 3: ....

3D **Complete the information about rodeos.**

A rodeo is a horse-riding and **1.**_____ festival. The most famous rodeos are in **2.**_____, USA. The origin is **3.**_____. In the early days of the Wild West, cowboy skills were very important. Cowboys practised their skills in **4.**_____. Buffalo **5.**_____ Cody was a showman. He organised rodeos with big **6.**_____. Today Houston, Texas has the biggest **7.**_____. People can go to the funfair, watch cowboys and cowgirls in competitions, ride **8.**_____, watch pig **9.**_____ and lots more.

3E **Answer the questions.**
1. How were the following natural wonders formed? Choose from: by erosion, by volcanic activity, by living organisms.

a. The Grand Canyon   ....
b. Giant's Causeway   ....
c. Old Faithful   ....
d. The Great Barrier Reef   ....
e. Uluru   ....

2. Give three examples of wear erosion.

1. ....
....
2. ....
....
3. ....
....

Crossing Cultures © ELI   Photocopiable

84

Name _____ Date: _____ Class _____

TEST - Block 4

4A Answer the questions.
1. How old are children when they start school in the USA? ....
2. What is the first year of school called in the USA? ....
3. What is the last year of school called in the USA? ....
4. How old are children when they start school in Ireland? ....
5. When can children leave school in Ireland? ....
6. What is a transition year in Ireland? ....

4B
1. Name 6 jobs that kids in the UK can do.
1. .... 3. .... 5. ....
2. .... 4. .... 6. ....

2. Complete the text about Craig Kielburger and Iqbal Masih.

When he was 12 years old, Canadian Craig Kielburger read a **1.**_____ story about a boy called Iqbal Masih. Iqbal was the same age as Craig, but lived in **2.**_____. His story is a terrible one. He was a **3.**_____ worker. When he protested about his **4.**_____ conditions and the conditions of other child workers, he was murdered. Craig was very **5.**_____ and decided to start a **6.**_____ to free child workers in the developing world. He and his classmates started an organization called '**7.**_____ The Children'. They **8.**_____ cars, they **9.**_____ cakes and they organized garage sales. They made money to help children like Iqbal. They also wrote to **10.**_____ all over the world and organized petitions. They tried to stop countries from buying products made by exploited **11.**_____. 'Free The Children' is still active today.

4C
1. Name 6 types of magazine.
1. .... 3. .... 5. ....
2. .... 4. .... 6. ....

2. Name 10 things you can find inside a magazine.
1. .... 5. .... 9. ....
2. .... 6. .... 10. ....
3. .... 7. ....
4. .... 8. ....

4D Answer the questions.
1. What languages did people speak in Britain before the fifth century? ....
2. What were the names of the three tribes which invaded Britain? ....
3. Where did they come from? ....
4. Where did the three tribes settle? ....
5. Which tribe had a language called "*Englisc*"? ....

4E Choose the correct answer.
1. Loch means
a) ☐ Scottish b) ☐ lake c) ☐ castle

2. Loch Ness is almost
a) ☐ 130 m deep b) ☐ 1,130 m deep c) ☐ 230 m deep

3. Loch Ness is near
a) ☐ Belfast b) ☐ Inverness c) ☐ London

4. Loch Ness is famous for
a) ☐ its fish b) ☐ its cake c) ☐ its monster

Photocopiable   Crossing Cultures © ELI

85

Name _____   Date: _____ Class _____

TEST - Block 5

5A

Name 3 disadvantages and 2 advantages of school uniform.	Name 5 rules related to school uniform.	Name 5 punishments used in schools in the English-speaking world.
1.	1.	1. ....
2.	2.	2. ....
3.	3.	3. ....
1.	4.	4. ....
2.	5.	5. ....

5B **Answer the questions.**

1. What time do Australians usually have their evening meal? ....
2. What do people in Australia usually drink with their evening meal? ....
3. How should you "mind your manners" in an Australian house? ....
4. What time do British people usually have their evening meal? ....
5. What do people in Britain usually drink with their evening meal? ....
6. How should you "mind your manners" in a British house? ....
7. What time do Americans usually have their evening meal? ....
8. What do people in America usually drink with their evening meal? ....
9. How should you "mind your manners" in an American house? ....

5C **Answer the questions.**

1. Name 2 pieces of equipment players use in baseball. ....
2. Name 2 pieces of equipment players use in cricket. ....
3. Name 2 pieces of equipment players use in American football. ....
4. Name a piece of equipment players use in Australian rules football. ....
5. What shape is the field in baseball? ....
6. How many players are there on a cricket team? ....
7. How many players are there on an American football team? ....
8. What do supporters shout at a cricket match? ....

5D **Are these sentences True or False?**   T   F

1. The Notting Hill Carnival is in February. ☐ ☐
2. Pancake day is the day before Lent begins. ☐ ☐
3. Scottish children sometimes roll eggs down hills at Easter. ☐ ☐
4. St. Patrick's day on March 17th is associated with the colour purple. ☐ ☐
5. Children sing and dance round a tadpole in May in the UK. ☐ ☐

5E **Answer the questions.**

1. Where did Charles Darwin come from? ....
2. What is he famous for? ....
3. Why was the black peppered moth more common than the white peppered moth during the industrial revolution? ....
4. Which of these animals is extinct?   a) ☐ panda   b) ☐ tiger   c) ☐ dodo.

Crossing Cultures © ELI   Photocopiable

86

Name _____   Date: _____   Class _____

TEST - Block 6

6A Choose the correct answer.

1066 was a very important year in **1.** *Ugandan / British* history. It was the end of the **2.** *Saxon / Medieval* era and the beginning of the **3.** *Noddyland / Norman* era. **4.** *Ernie / Edward* the Confessor, the last Saxon King died in January **5.** *1966 / 1066*. There were three possible successors to the throne: Harold Godwin (Saxon), Harold Hardrada (Viking King of Norway) and William of **6.** *Normandy / Tuscany*. The three men had large **7.** *armies / sleevies*. There were several battles in the summer. The final battle was the Battle of **8.** *Little Big Horn / Hastings* when William of Normandy defeated Harold Godwin. This was a turning point in British history.

6B Part one:

1. Name four types of room you can find in a house.
   ....
2. Name two types of unusual home.
   ....
3. Name one advantage and one disadvantage of living in a lighthouse.
   ....

Part two:
Describe your house or flat.
....
....
....
....

6C Answer the questions.

1. Name 3 eras when the yo-yo was a popular craze.
2. Name 3 other types of crazes through the ages.
3. What equipment do you need for skateboarding?
4. Name 4 chess pieces.

....
....
....
....

6D Part one:
Imagine you are going to travel on a steamship to America. Answer the following questions:

1. What are you going to take with you?
   ....
2. What are you going to do on your journey?
   ....
3. What are you going to miss when you arrive?
   ....

Part two:
Complete the letter home.

Dear _____
We are now in America. The ship was _____.
We _____ on the journey.
I really miss _____ and _____.
I'll write again soon
love from
_____

6E Part one:
Answer the questions.

1. Who was Neil Armstrong?
   ....
2. What famous mountain was first climbed in 1953?
   ....
3. In which river was the first ever submarine trip?
   ....
4. Who was the first person to reach the South Pole?
   ....

Part two:
Fill the blanks in the text. Use the first letters to help you.

In 1911, there were two expeditions to the **1.** S_____ P_____. One was **2.** N_____ led by the famous explorer Roald Amundsen. It started from The Bay of Whales in October 1911. The second expedition, led by the **3.** B_____ explorer Robert Scott started a month later in **4.** N_____ 1911 from Cape Evans. The two teams followed different routes. Amundsen reached the Transantarctic **5.** M_____ in November 1911 and Scott reached the same mountains in December 1911. Amundsen reached the South Pole in December 1911 and Scott arrived 33 days later in **6.** J_____ 1912. Amundsen's successful expedition returned to base camp. Scott's mission was a disaster. All the members of the team **7.** d_____ on the return journey. Scott himself died in March 1912.

Photocopiable   Crossing Cultures © ELI

Name _____   Date: _____   Class _____

TEST - Block 7

7A **Answer the questions.**

1. Which of these schools is a state school in the UK?
   a) ☐ prep school   b) ☐ public school   c) ☐ comprehensive school
2. Name one famous person who went to Eton College School.
   ....
3. Name 3 things which Roald Dahl kept in his tuck box.
   ....
4. Write a list of 10 things to keep in your tuck box.
   ....

7B **1. Name ten electrical items you have in your house.**
   ....
   ....

2. Name three things which didn't exist in the 1950s.
   ....

7C **Choose the correct answer.**

The London 1908 Olympics was the **1.** *fourth / twentieth* Olympic Games. It was the **2.** *first / last* time that all the athletes marched into the stadium together – all **3.** *240 / 22* nations. There were 2,008 athletes taking part in the Games - 1,971 men and **4.** *437 / 37* women. There were 110 events in total. The new events for 1908 included **5.** *ice-skating / snowboarding*. The fastest time for the men's 100m was 10.8 seconds (Reggie Walker from South Africa). **6.** *The Solomon Islands / the USA* won the most medals (35). The most successful individual athletes were Henry Taylor from Britain (3 gold medals in **7.** *swimming / cooking*) and Mel Shepherd from the USA (3 medals in athletics).

7D **Are these sentences True or False?**

	T	F
1. Captain Cook's first name was James.	☐	☐
2. He studied maths and astronomy.	☐	☐
3. Cook was a Master and Commander in the Royal Air Force.	☐	☐
4. He made the first maps of Newfoundland.	☐	☐
5. He drew maps of Iceland and Greenland.	☐	☐
6. He was killed in 1969.	☐	☐

7E **Write about a building that you like. Explain where it is, what it's for and why you like it.**

....
....
....
....
....
....
....
....
....

Name _____   Date: _____ Class _____

TEST - Block 8

8A Answer the questions.

1. Name three acid substances.   1. .... 2. .... 3. ....
2. Name three alkaline substances.   1. .... 2. .... 3. ....
3. What substance is neither acid nor alkaline?   ....
4. What colour is neutral on the pH scale?   ....
5. Which is more acidic, soap flakes or cola?   ....
6. What colour is acid on the pH scale?   ....

8B

Part one
Write five good things about living in a big city.
....
....

Write five good things about living in a small town.
....
....
....

Part two
Write about the advantages and disadvantages of the place where you live.
....
....
....
....
....

8C Write a paragraph about your favourite film. Say why you like it.

....
....
....

8D Fill the blanks in the text. Use the first letter of the word to help you.

In America until the 1960s and in South Africa until the 1990s, society was **1.** r_____. Black people couldn't **2.** e___ in the same restaurants as white people; they couldn't **3.** w___ down the street with a white person. Black and white people sat in different places on **4.** b___ and used different entrances in **5.** c_____. There were different **6.** s_____ for black and white people. Black people often couldn't **7.** v___. In America and in South Africa there were protest campaigns to get equality for black and white people. Two great leaders of these campaigns were **8.** M____ L____ K___ and **9.** N___ M____.

8E

Part one
1. Name five reasons why London was a horrible place to live in the nineteenth century.
....
....
....
....
....

2. Write five adjectives to describe a foggy day.
....
....

Part two
Write about a foggy day.
....
....
....
....
....
....
....
....
....

Photocopiable   Crossing Cultures © ELI

Name _____   Date: _____   Class _____

TEST - Block 9

9A Write a paragraph about studying English abroad. Say where you would like to study and why.

....
....
....
....
....
....
....

9B Fill the blanks with the correct religion.

1. The menorah is a symbol of the _____ faith.
2. The cross is a symbol of the _____ faith.
3. The Omkar is a symbol of _____.
4. The Dharma is a symbol of _____.
5. The crescent and star is a symbol of _____.
6. The Khanda is a symbol of _____.

9C Part one
Make a list of fashionable and unfashionable clothes.

FASHIONABLE	UNFASHIONABLE

Part two
Describe what you are wearing today.

....
....
....
....
....
....

9D Answer the questions.

1. When was the English Civil War?
   ....
2. Who did Cavaliers fight for?
   ....
3. Who was the leader of Parliament?
   ....
4. What happened to the king?
   ....

9E Are these sentences True or False?

                T   F

1. Most cotton plantations in America were in the North of the USA. ☐ ☐
2. Cotton was picked and cleaned by machines. ☐ ☐
3. It was a very easy job. ☐ ☐
4. A bale of cotton weighs less than 300 kg. ☐ ☐
5. From one bale of cotton you can make 1,200 T-shirts. ☐ ☐
6. Cotton is important in America today. ☐ ☐

Crossing Cultures © ELI   Photocopiable

Name _____ Date: _____ Class _____

TEST - Block 10

10A **Part one**
Name five famous sights in New York City.

1. ....
2. ....
3. ....
4. ....
5. ....

Part two
Write about your journey home from school.

....
....
....
....
....

10B Answer the questions.

1. What language do the Amish speak? ....
2. Do Amish children go to school? ....
3. Why don't the Amish use electricity or cars? ....
4. Do the Amish play musical instruments? ....
5. Do Amish children play games? ....
6. Is the Amish calendar the same as ours? ....

10C Write about your favourite band or musician. Say why you like them.

....
....
....

10D Fill the blanks in the text. Use the first letter of the word to help you.

In the USA things are different: the individual states have a lot of power. For example, some states have the **1.** d____ penalty, some states don't. The American **2.** C_____ says how the American government works. The government is divided into **3.** t____ sections. These are the **4.** E_____ Branch, the **5.** L_____ Branch and the **6.** J_____ Branch. The head of the Executive Branch is the **7.** p_____. The president has a cabinet of ministers. The head of the Legislative Branch is **8.** C_____. In Congress, there are two chambers, the **9.** S_____ and the House of **10.** R_____.

10E Which of these inventions do you think is the most important?

the wheel	the computer	the car	the printing press	television	the plane

Write a paragraph explaining why.

....
....
....
....
....
....

Answers to Tests

1A
1. a) by b) on
2. Any 8 forms of transport are acceptable.
3. The students will probably choose from those mentioned in the lesson - Australia, Canada, the USA, Britain and Ireland, though there are other countries in the world where the mile is used.
4. 1.6 km = 1 mile

1B
1. *wash / clean* the car
2. *feed* the fish
3. *clean* the bathroom
4. *lay* the table
5. *cut* the grass
6. *make* the bed
7. *do* the ironing
8. *take out* the rubbish

1C
1. a) astronomer (accept astronomy)
   b) interpreter (accept interpreting)
   c) meteorologist (accept meteorology)
   d) camp cook (accept cooking, or chef)
   e) artist (accept art or drawing or illustrating)
   f) canoeist (accept canoeing)
   g) climber (accept climbing)
   h) entertainer
2. Answer d), map-reading

1D
1. Ireland, 2. October, 3. candle, 4. Celts, 5. winter, 6. houses, 7. trick, 8. sweets.

1E

ANIMAL	COUNTRY	ADJECTIVE
Koala	Australia	various answers possible
Skunk	USA	various answers possible
Katipo	New Zealand	various answers possible
Giant galliwasp	Caribbean	various answers possible
Bobcat	North America	various answers possible
Kiwi	New Zealand	various answers possible
Cobra	India	various answers possible

2A
1. Physical Education.
2. Hockey.
3. Accept any 6 sports that use a ball.
4. Accept any 3 sports where you hit a ball.
5. Accept any 3 sports where you throw a ball.

2B
Free answer.

2C
The ten types of television programme mentioned in the lesson are: docudramas, reality shows, soaps, news, quiz shows, sports programmes, food programmes, sitcoms, cartoons and music programmes. Other answers may be possible.

2D
1. Seven years of bad luck
2. All your luck will fall out
3. Four
4. Salute it
5. Yes
6. At New Year

2E
1. hurricanes, 2. tornadoes, 3. clouds, 4. winds, 5. anticlockwise, 6. clockwise, 7. one/1, 8. five/5, 9. August, 10. New Orleans.

3A
1. Accept any 5 summer camp activities – those mentioned in the lesson are: mountain biking, tennis, drama, arts and crafts, photography, baseball, sailing, canoeing, fishing, surfing, swimming, water-skiing, horse-riding, cowboy skills, rodeo, trail-riding, animal care, gardening.
2. Free answer.

3B
Free answer.

3C
1. Various answers are possible
2. Choose from: always queue up; give the money to the shop assistant; always say please and thank you; never ask for two of something by sticking up two fingers.

3D
1. cowboy; 2. Texas; 3. Spanish; 4. competitions; 5. Bill; 6. prizes; 7. rodeo; 8. horses; 9. races.

3E
1. a) erosion b) erosion c) volcanic activity d) living organisms e) erosion
2. Various answers are possible. Those mentioned in the book are: coins, shoes and pencils.

4A
1. six 2. first grade 3. twelfth grade 4. four 5. sixteen 6. a year when students do special courses.

4B
1. Choose from: hairdresser, car wash attendant, waiter / waitress, paper boy or girl, shop assistant, farm worker, hotel cleaner / chambermaid, working with animals.
2. 1. newspaper 2. Pakistan 3. slave 4. working 5. angry 6. campaign 7. Free 8. washed 9. made 10. politicians 11. children

4C
Choose from:
1. celebrity gossip, sports, car and motorbike, travel, tv and radio listings, fashion, music, hobbies and interests, science. Other answers may be possible.
2. crossword & puzzle page, letters page, gossip, interview, cartoons, contents, special feature articles, questionnaires & quizzes, experiment, games, Q and A, readers' club.
Other answers may be possible.

4D
1. Celtic 2. Angles, Saxons, Jutes 3. Denmark and Northern Germany 4. Angles in the East, Jutes in the South and Saxons in the South East 5. Angles.

4E
1. b; 2. c; 3. b; 4. c.

5A
Choose from:
Disadvantages:
Some uniforms are expensive.
Ties are really uncomfortable.
Girls look really stupid in ties.
Everyone looks the same.
Uniforms are really old-fashioned.

Advantages:
Rich and poor kids look the same.
You don't have to decide what to wear in the morning.

Rules:
No make-up
No big jewellery
No trainers
No short skirts
No collars up
No big ties
No top button undone
No blazers inside out

Punishments:
lines – writing words or sentences many times
detention – staying after school for an hour

exclusion – being suspended from school
a telling-off – the teacher is angry with you
extra homework
standing outside the classroom
isolation booths – you work alone for the day
a phone call informing parents

5B
1. about six; 2. water, beer, wine; 3. offer to help clear up and tidy away after a meal; 4. from five to eight; 5. tea, coffee, juice, milk; 6. say 'please' and 'thank you'; 7. it varies; 8. iced water, milk, fruit juice; 9. don't start eating straight away.

5C
1. Choose from: bat, gloves, helmet, ball
2. Choose from: bat, ball, pads, helmet, gloves
3. Choose from: ball, pads, helmet, gloves
4. ball
5. a diamond
6. eleven
7. fifty-three
8. 'Howzat?'

5D
1. False 2. True 3. True 4. False 5. False

5E
1. Britain 2. Theory of evolution 3. Because of pollution 4. c

6A
1. British; 2. Saxon; 3. Norman; 4. Edward; 5. 1066; 6. Normandy; 7. armies; 8. Hastings.

6B
Part one:
1. Choose from those mentioned in the lesson (listed below) or any other acceptable rooms in a house: bedroom, games room, bathroom, living room, kitchen.
2. Choose from those mentioned in the lesson (listed below) – other answers may be possible: lighthouse, windmill, horse-drawn caravan.
3 Advantage: it's on the beach. Disadvantage: there are lots of steps
Part two: free answer.

6C
1. Choose three from the following eras:
Ancient Greece around 500 BC
Ancient Egypt around 1100 BC
16th century Philippines
French Revolution era 1788 – 1804
The Napoleonic Age 1793 – 1815
The Space Age 1957 – today
2. Choose three from: chess, marbles, Rubik's cube, skipping, hula hoop, roller skating, rollerblading, cycling.
3. helmet, knee pads, elbow pads, trainers, wrist-guards.
4. Choose four from: pawn, castle / rook, knight, bishop, queen, king.

6D
Part one: free answers.
Part two: free answer.

6E
Part one:
1. He was an astronaut, 2. Everest, 3. The river Thames, 4. Amundsen.
Part two:
1. South Pole, 2. Norwegian, 3. British, 4. November, 5. Mountains, 6. January, 7. died.

7A
1. c) 2. Choose from: Shelley, Princes William and Harry, James Bond.
3. Choose from: half a cake, a packet of squashed fly biscuits, a couple of oranges, an apple, a banana, a pot of strawberry jam, a bar of chocolate, a bag of liquorice allsorts, a tin of Bassett's lemonade powder. 4. Free answer.

7B
1. Free answer, 2. Free answer.

7C
1. fourth, 2. first, 3. twenty-two, 4. thirty-seven 5. ice-skating, 6. the USA, 7. swimming

7D
1. True, 2. True, 3. False, 4. True, 5. False, 6. False

7E
Free answer.

8A
1. Choose from: stomach acid, lemon juice, vinegar, cola, tomato juice, tea, black coffee, milk.
2. Choose from: oven cleaner, soap flakes, household ammonia, bleach, milk of magnesia.
3. water
4. green
5. cola
6. red

8B
Part one: free answer.
Part two: free answer.

8C
Free answer.

8D
1. racist, 2. eat, 3. walk, 4. buses, 5. cinemas, 6. schools, 7. vote, 8. Martin Luther King, 9. Nelson Mandela.

8E
Part one:
1. Choose from: pickpockets, child labour, prison, the workhouse, the river, the smell, pestilence, fog. Other answers may be possible.
2. Choose from: damp, smoky, freezing, depressing. Other answers may be possible.
Part two: free answer.

9A
Free answer.

9B
1. Jewish, 2. Christian, 3. Hinduism, 4. Buddhism, 5. Islam, 6. Sikhism

9C
Part one: free answer.
Part two: free answer.

9D
1. 1642 to 1651, 2. The King, 3. Oliver Cromwell, 4. Executed.

9E
1. False, 2. False, 3. False, 4. True, 5. True, 6. True.

10A
Part one:
Choose from: Times Square, Brooklyn Bridge, The Empire State Building, Central Park, The Statue of Liberty, Broadway, Little Italy. Other answers may be possible.
Part two: free answer.

10B
1. Pennsylvania Dutch, 2. Yes, 3. They are unnecessary, 4. No, 5. Yes, 6. Yes.

10C
Free answer.

10D
1. death, 2. Constitution, 3. three, 4. Executive, 5. Legislative, 6. Judicial, 7. president, 8. Congress, 9. Senate, 10. Representatives.

10E
Free answer.

CD-ROMs Answer Keys to printable texts

School Life and Education

Hogwarts

Comprehension
1. 1000 AD. 2. Scotland. 3. By owl. 4. Four. 5. Sixteen. 6. Yes. 7. Pumpkin juice. 8. Yes.

Summary skills
Hogwarts is a special school in <u>Scotland</u> for witches and wizards. The most famous student in the school is <u>Harry Potter</u>. Students don't study traditional school <u>subjects</u>. They <u>study</u> things like Potions and Transfiguration, instead. Students like the <u>food</u>, especially cakes, pies and sausages and they have <u>feasts</u> on special occasions. The <u>uniform</u> at Hogwarts is black.

Eating junk

Comprehension
1. Bread, rice, pasta and potatoes. 2. Five. 3. Choose from: hamburgers, chips, crisps, chocolate. 4. They have a lot of sugar in them. 5. Snacks like crisps and chocolate, colas and other sugary drinks. 6. Frozen junk food like chips, burgers and hot dogs. 7. Because it's cheap to make. 8. No.

Summary skills
1. A healthy diet; 2. What is junk food?; 3. Junk food snacks in schools; 4. School lunches; 5. Is tomato ketchup a vegetable?

Schools in the cinema *(Pre-reading)*

Comprehension
1. Drama, comedy, musical, science-fiction, fantasy and documentary. 2. In 1978. 3. 23 and 27. 4. The Plastics. 5. Jack Black. 6. He's a teacher. 7. Michael Moore. 8. An Oscar.

Summary skills
1. Musical – Grease 2. Comedy – Mean Girls 3. Documentary – Bowling for Columbine 4. Comedy – School of Rock

High School in the USA *(Pre-reading)*

Comprehension
1. 14 or 15 years old. 2. Science, mathematics, English, social science and some physical education. 3. History and economics. 4. Subjects students choose to study. 5. Choose from: computing, athletics, foreign languages, performing arts or visual arts. 6. Drama, dance, singing or orchestra. 7. In the last two years of high school. 8. So they can play for their school teams.

Summary skills
1. High schools in the USA 2. Basic school subjects 3. Electives 4. Special classes for 'gifted' students 5. Extra activities after school

Stop bullies! *(Pre-reading)*

Comprehension
1. Boys and girls who are horrible to other people. 2. Choose from: they say horrible things, they are violent, they take things, they send horrible messages, they ignore people. 3. No. It's not your fault. 4. Family, teachers, classmates. 5. The bully will probably continue to hurt you. 6. So you can remember the details when you tell someone. 7. So they don't get into really big trouble in the future.

Summary skills
1. Tell someone. 2. Talk to teachers. 3. Keep calm. 4. Make a list of the things the bully does. 5. Stay in a group.

People and Lifestyles

Job Ideas for Teens *(Pre-reading)*

Comprehension
1. Because Saturday is the busiest day of the week for many shops and restaurants. 2. Gardening and babysitting. 3. Three. 4. Walking, washing and looking after them when the family is on holiday. 5. Newspaper. 6. Party organiser.

Summary skills
1. domestic animals – pets; journalists – reporters; people who live near you – neighbours; parents – mum and dad; shopping centre – mall. 2. It's very ~~difficult~~ *easy* to get a Saturday job, because Saturday is a busy day for businesses. You could work in a ~~bank~~ *shop* or a restaurant. You could do babysitting or ~~driving~~ *gardening*. If you want to start a business, it's easier to do it ~~alone~~ *if there is a group of you*. You could take ~~cats~~ *dogs* for a walk, you could start a community ~~TV station~~ *newspaper* and, if you are good at ~~dancing~~ *cooking*, you could organize children's parties.

What's the best pet for you? *(Pre-reading)*

Comprehension
1. Cats. 2. 260. 3. They need special food and warm temperatures. 4. 21. 5. A dog. 6. Dogs, cats, a tortoise, guinea pigs and hamsters. 7. Grass, hay, apples. 8. Fish.

Summary skills
1. The most popular pet 2. The most unusual pet – tarantula 3. The oldest pet 4. The student with the most pets 5. The biggest pet 6. The smallest pet

Sydney: Australia's favourite city *(Pre-reading)*

Comprehension
1. More than 4 million. 2. The Sydney Harbour Bridge and the Sydney Opera House. 3. Warm. 4. In the financial district. 5. Near the Harbour. 6. The UK, China, Italy and the Philippines. 7. Because they can go to the beach in the daytime and enjoy the restaurants and nightclubs in the evening. 8. On 31st December.

Summary skills
Sydney is Australia's largest city with a population of <u>4 million</u>. It has two very famous landmarks <u>Sydney Harbour Bridge</u> and <u>the Sydney Opera House</u>. In Sydney, the weather is <u>warm</u> in January and <u>cold</u> in July. In Sydney, there are many immigrants from many different countries, including the UK, China, <u>Italy</u> and the Philippines. Sydney is also popular with <u>tourists</u>. They like the beaches and the nightlife. Sydney is a popular destination for the New Year and there is a big fireworks display on <u>31st December</u>.

The Spelling Bee *(Pre-reading)*

Comprehension
1. Because there are a lot of exceptions to spelling rules and they are very difficult to remember. 2. There are special activity books and spelling tests. 3. In America. 4. They buy special books. 5. In 1925. 6. Up to $22,000. 7. Books, dictionaries, scholarships and prizes for their schools.

Summary skills
English spelling is very ~~easy~~ *difficult*. To help children learn to spell, schools have special books, tests and spelling ~~spiders~~ *bees*. Spelling bees are competitions. They are usually for ~~adults~~ *children*. These competitions are sometimes international. Children can win up to ~~25 cents~~ *$22,000*.

Maori History and Culture (Pre-reading)

Comprehension
1. Polynesia. 2. By canoe. 3. By hunting and fishing. 4. On European ships. 5. In 1840. 6. English and Maori. 7. They often have no jobs and there are problems with racism.

Summary skills
1. The first inhabitants of New Zealand 2. Maori meet Europeans 3. The Effect of the British Empire 4. Maori Life and Culture Today

Sport and Leisure

The Friendly Games (Pre-reading)

Comprehension
1. Every four years; 2. The Friendly Games; 3. 53; 4. 16; 5. No; 6. In 1930; 7. Two weeks.

Summary skills
1. What are the Commonwealth Games? 2. What is the Commonwealth? 3. What sports are there in the Commonwealth Games? 4. Do people watch the games on TV? 5. How long do the games last? 6. Where are the Commonwealth Games usually held?

Mobiles in the English Speaking World (Pre-reading)

Comprehension
1. They were expensive and heavy; 2. 13 million; 3. £300 a year; 4. Three quarters; 5. 50 million; 6. 10%; 7. Mobile phones; 8. Parents.

Summary skills
Thirteen million young people in Britain have a ~~television~~ *mobile phone*. Some teenagers spend a lot of money on their phones – about ~~30p~~ *£300* a year. ~~7%~~ *75%* of teenagers used their phones in an emergency. In the USA, about ~~9 million~~ *50 million* young people have cell phones. They spend more on phones than they spend on ~~bowling~~ *sweets and music*. Almost ~~100 per cent~~ *90%* of teenagers aged between 13 and 19 in Sydney and Melbourne have mobile phones.

Reality Show Crazy (Pre-reading)

Comprehension
1. In Holland. 2. George Orwell. 3. 1984. 4. "I'm a Celebrity Get me out of Here". 5. Money or modelling work. 6. Pop Idol. 7. 70%.

Summary skills
Big Brother was the first big reality show. It started in Holland. ~~Holland is also called The Netherlands.~~ The idea came from a character in George Orwell's 1984 called Big Brother. ~~George Orwell went to live in India.~~ Other famous reality shows follow celebrities or people who want to be models and singers. ~~Kate Moss is a famous model.~~

All about hip hop (Pre-reading)

Comprehension
1. Rap, graffiti and break dancing. 2. In the 1970s. 3. In the Bronx, New York. 4. The MC and the DJ. 5. In New York. 6. Yes. 7. No.

Newspapers in Britain and America (Pre-reading)

Comprehension
1. Red tops. 2. The Sun and The Mirror. 3. The Guardian, The Times and The Independent. 4. Home and world news, economics, sports, films, music and politics. 5. The Wall Street Journal and The Washington Post. 6. Time Out. 7. Time and Newsweek. 8. Cinema, theatre and exhibition reviews.

Summary skills
1. Red Tops 2. Qualities 3. Listings Magazines 4. Weeklies

History and Traditions

The Statue of Liberty: a symbol of freedom (Pre-reading)

Comprehension
1. New York; 2. 50 m; 3. 5 m; 4. France; 5. A torch and a tablet; 6. No; 7. A museum; 8. 354; 9. The Day After Tomorrow and Spiderman II.

Summary skills
The Statue of Liberty is a symbol of American freedom and independence. It's in New York on a small island in the Hudson River. ~~The Hudson River is 485 km long.~~ The Statue of Liberty is almost 50 m tall. It was a gift from France in 1885. ~~The capital of France is Paris.~~ Tourists can visit the statue and museum 364 days a year. ~~Christmas Day is 25th December.~~ The Statue of Liberty is so famous you can see it in lots of films.

St. Patrick: the Patron Saint of Ireland (Pre-reading)

Comprehension
1. It's St. Patrick's Day. 2. In the fifth century. 3. He was captured and sold as a slave. 4. In Gaul. 5. St. Patrick. 6. Parades. 7. Guinness and Irish whiskey. 8. In New York.

Summary skills
St. Patrick is the Patron Saint of ~~Scotland~~ *Ireland*. Patrick lived in the ~~nineteenth~~ *fifth century*. He went to Ireland as a slave. He escaped and went to ~~India~~ *Gaul*. He returned to Ireland as a ~~bus driver~~ *priest*. Today people celebrate St. Patrick's Day on 17th ~~December~~ *March*. They have parades in the street and have parties in pubs. People also celebrate St. ~~Peter~~ *Patrick's* Day in America and other countries.

Rosa Parks and segregation (Pre-reading)

Comprehension
1. Separating white and black people. 2. Voting laws were strict. 3. White people sat at the front of buses and blacks sat at the back. 4. In a department store. 5. She was angry about segregation and the arrest of a young girl. 6. The police arrested her. 7. A bus boycott. 8. In 2005.

Summary skills
1. Segregation in the USA 2. Segregation on buses 3. Rosa Parks and the bus boycott 4. Rosa Parks' later years

Bonfire Night, Guy Fawkes and the Gunpowder Plot *(Pre-reading)*

Comprehension
1. On November 5th. 2. In 1605. 3. King James I. 4. The Houses of Parliament. 5. A letter telling him not to go to the Houses of Parliament. 6. In a cellar under the Houses of Parliament. 7. He was tortured and executed. 8. Albus Dumbledore.

Summary skills
1. They wanted to kill the Queen and her family. 2. He was making a cake for the King.

What's Lucky, What's Unlucky? *(Pre-reading)*

Comprehension
1. Bees, black cats, sheep and dolphins. 2. Apples. 3. Count the pips in half an apple. 4. Oil and salt. 5. Inside the house. 6. A hat. 7. Yellow. 8. A pot of gold.

Summary skills
1. Animals 2. Food 3. Inside the house 4. Sport 5. Weather

The world we live in

Muncaster Castle and its ghosts *(Pre-reading)*

Comprehension
1. In the Lake District, Cumbria. 2. Because of its ghosts. 3. Pennington. 4. It's expensive to live in a castle. 5. Fortress. 6. Tom Fool and Mary Bragg. 7. They turn on and off. 8. Owls.

Summary skills
1. Where is Muncaster? 2. Who lives there? 3. Buildings at the castle 4. Muncaster's ghosts 5. Owls and the World Owl Trust

Niagara Falls: facts and figures *(Pre-reading)*

Comprehension
1. On the border between Canada and the USA. 2. Two. 3. By a bridge. 4. Yes. 5. From a tunnel. 6. Yes. 7. Water stopped flowing over the falls / the river froze.

Summary skills
Niagara Falls is ~~one~~ *a group* of famous waterfalls on the border between the USA and ~~Mexico~~ *Canada*. They are about a ~~metre~~ *kilometre* long. There are two towns called Niagara Falls, ~~both~~ *one* is in the USA and the other is in Canada. Tourists ~~can't~~ see the falls from a helicopter or a cable car and there ~~isn't~~ a boat trip on the River Niagara. Tourists ~~can't~~ visit the falls at night because ~~there aren't any lights~~ they are illuminated. The falls ~~stop flowing every March~~ *stopped flowing for two days in March 1848*.

Canada's National Symbols *(Pre-reading)*

Comprehension
1. The bald eagle. 2. New Zealand. 3. The maple leaf and the moose. 4. Elk. 5. Trees and grass. 6. 820 kg. 7. The maple leaf. 8. Syrup, sugar and sweets.

Summary skills
~~No~~ *Most* countries have national symbols like animals, birds and flowers. Canada has two important symbols, the ~~dog~~ *moose* and the maple leaf. Moose live in ~~cities~~ *forests*. They eat ~~burgers and chips~~ *wood from trees and grass*. A lot of maple products are made in Canada. Examples are maple sugar, maple ~~sauce~~ *syrup* and maple sweets.

Scotland: the land of inventors *(Pre-reading)*

Comprehension
1. 5 million. 2. Dunlop. 3. In 1888. 4. The decimal point. 5. Meat and vegetables. 6. Golf. 7. Sir Alexander Fleming. 8. She was the first cloned mammal.

Summary skills
There are a lot of famous Scottish inventors. ~~Scotland is north of England.~~ They invented things like the telephone, the steam engine, pneumatic tyres and the fridge. ~~You should clean your fridge often.~~ They also made important scientific discoveries and inventions like the decimal point, penicillin and cloning. The Scottish also invented golf. ~~Golfers traditionally wear colourful socks.~~

The Taj Mahal: a monument to love *(Pre-reading)*

Comprehension
1. In India. 2. The Yamuna River. 3. Shah Jahan. 4. Mumtaz Mahal. 5. In 1631. 6. White marble. 7. 22,000. 8. Five times a month.

Summary skills
1. Where is the Taj Mahal? 2. The Love Story behind the Taj Mahal 3. Building the Taj Mahal 4. Visiting the Taj Mahal